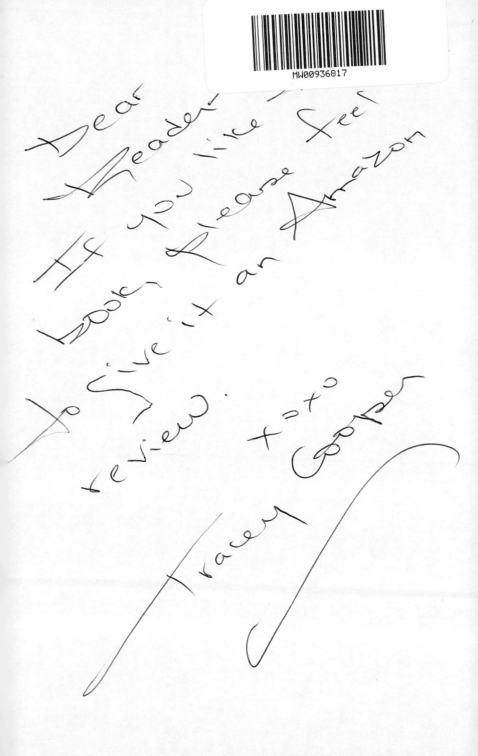

Dear Reader,

If you like this book, please feel free to give it an Amazon review.

$x=x^o$

Cooper

Tracey

JOCKEY DAUGHTER

JOCKEY DAUGHTER

I Do Not Have to Be Beaten to Cross the Finish Line

TRACEY COOPER

JOCKEY DAUGHTER
I DO NOT HAVE TO BE BEATEN TO CROSS THE FINISH LINE

iUniverse books may be ordered through booksellers or by contacting:

iUniverse
1663 Liberty Drive
Bloomington, IN 47403
www.iuniverse.com
1-800-Authors (1-800-288-4677)

ISBN: 978-1-5320-0438-4 (sc)
ISBN: 978-1-5320-0440-7 (hc)
ISBN: 978-1-5320-0439-1 (e)

Library of Congress Control Number: 2016915052

Print information available on the last page.

iUniverse rev. date: 10/5/2016

To my beautiful daughter and son whom I adore. Placing one thousand kisses upon their heads seemed like not enough. From the moment of their births, I vowed to love them, protect them, respect them, and cherish them. My vow included an absence of physical and or emotional trauma to their bodies and souls. They are my greatest gift to myself, my most worthy and satisfying accomplishment.

To my four sisters and two brothers, who are the added witnesses to the events in this book. We were graced with good looks, charm, and intelligence, but as children we were held in a daily bondage of familial contempt, anger, and resentment. Our aging set us free. My siblings were so strong and so loyal during the toughest of moments. I admire their fortitude and strength more than my own.

And to those who experience the same pain within their family settings. My head is bowed, and my hope for you is that you too find success in having a purposeful and peaceful life filled with laughter and love. You, too, know that you do not have to be beaten to cross the finish line.

CONTENTS

PREFACE

WHEN THE IDEA TO WRITE this book kept surfacing in my mind, I initially thought that bookshelves did not need another "I was physically abused book." While preparing to begin my writing, I was not sure it would cure any defect from the residual effects of my own childhood trauma. Then I began to write memories down in a notebook, and I realized that the events were indelible impressions in my mind and that writing them down was like putting them in a special drawer that I could lock. By locking the drawer that held these memories, I was able to step away from them. And I hope that by sharing them and my process, I might help someone else step away from his or her own traumas and come, as I have, to live a productive life.

In our home, the abusive events were oddly intertwined with the very public aspect of the professional "sport of kings" and the sheer excitement and magnitude of the horse racing industry. With our father driving race horses across the finish line, we were in a position to observe and live among Kentucky Derby winners, Preakness winners, Belmont Stakes winners, and Breeders' Cup champions. As children, my siblings and I needed to strike a balance between that public world and the private terror of consistent abuse by our own mother that we were experiencing at home. As adults, we needed to strike a different balance. We needed to face the bad memories head on and demand that they retreat to the back of our minds so that we could erase as much of the pain as we could and live fully in the present—a present in which none of us had repeated the abuse we'd been dealt as children. We had been stuck recalling some of the childhood scenes and trying to understand our mother for her unhealthy coping mechanisms composed of beating and verbally abusing us.

While adoring fans were cheering our father across the horse racing finish line, our mother was beating us within an inch of our lives. We endured her unbelievable anger, resentment, and negative energy. Each of us, upon turning eighteen years of age, either ran out the door or began a pursuit to get out the door. Five of us ended relationships through divorce. Astoundingly, none of us abuse our own precious children. None of us punched or beat or whipped our beautiful offspring. None of us used words that would scar their developing egos or weaken their souls.

As I proofread *Jockey Daughter*, I purposefully referred to the woman who raised us as "our mother." I simply could not give her a personal tie to me alone by calling her "my mother." Just as I found it impossible to say, "I love you" to her, it is impossible to use the word *my*, as doing so would solidify that she was mine. I certainly do not want to own her. I try hard not to remind myself that her DNA oozes through my blood. And I abhor the fact that I cannot excise from my cells the parts that come from her.

Writing this book opened a seal, exposing a truth that had remained hidden—and in that way, it was a vindication for every time we were asked, "How is your wonderful mother?" every time we were told to tell our "amazing mother" hello, and every time we observed her receiving cheers and accolades from our community church. She must own her actions. Hiding them in some repressed memory bank does not give title to those actions. She has never once apologized. She has never once reflected on the damage she thrust upon us. She has never once looked herself in the mirror and asked herself why on earth she lashed out. She is a coward and a hypocrite.

For children, it is impossible to modify the behavior of adults and almost equally as impossible to seek shelter from those who are harming you if they are the ones labeled parents. As youngsters, my siblings and I surely could not have done anything to shield ourselves. Today, doctors, teachers, and other individuals are encouraged to report any suspicions of abuse. This is a good start but not a complete finish. I think the onus of providing protection lies with those closer to the abused. Relatives and friends are in the best position to remove children from life-altering trauma or to at least call the abuser out. They must act on their instincts and antennae. The laws are in place to protect the most vulnerable. Now is the perfect time to make the call or to start the process of protection. No one needs to be beaten to cross life's finish line.

CHAPTER ONE

———◆———

AJAX CLEANSER AND A ROUND DIAMOND

AT AGE FIFTY-EIGHT, IT IS still impossible for me to look at Ajax cleanser or a round diamond.

I clearly remember the first time I felt terror. I was six years old, and my four-year-old sister, Mitzy, was in the kitchen of our 1961 custom-built, brick colonial. On the first floor of this home was a large kitchen adjacent to an entrance to and from the garage. Through the kitchen was a laundry room on one side; a wood-paneled family room on the other side; and a small area that served as the dining room, which always seemed to boast ghastly wall coverings. Thirteen stairs from the front hall foyer led to the second floor, with four bedrooms, a hall bath, and one master bedroom bath. There was a powder room on the first floor. The three bathrooms were all "period" selected, colorfully tiled rooms. There was the pink bathroom, the blue bathroom, and the green bathroom. The second-floor green bathroom was designated as the children's bath.

Standing on a former hog farm, our family home was alone within a densely wooded area of Laurel, Maryland. It was in the deeper section reserved for future homes, and a long, winding dirt road provided the only access to the property. As the first home to be built in this development, ours was isolated from the populated density of a large town or city. In other words, we lived alone in the woods.

Many neighborhoods in the 1960s incorporated racial covenants to prevent minority home ownership, and this development was no different. The restrictions added to the isolation from a growing minority population in the surrounding areas. The races were segregated by area. Blacks lived in black neighborhoods, and whites lived in white neighborhoods. Miscegenation laws were alive and well. God help you if you were white and in the private company of a black man.

Our development, through racial covenants, created separation due to the developer's vision for the community. The developer, presumably, was a member of the Ku Klux Klan, and he made sure that no minority, especially a black person, would reside anywhere near his home, which he occupied at the top of the neighborhood. He visited our home many times and made a point to always use the "n" word. Those ideals were not the ideals of my parents. They just could not get around the sign of the times.

On this particular day, as a small six-year-old, I was on the toilet in the green bathroom daydreaming and urinating, my feet dangling, not quite able to reach the green ceramic tile below me. As I sat on the toilet innocently singing in my head, I heard a bloodcurdling scream from my four-year-old sister, Mitzy, who had been on the first floor when I'd left her to climb the stairs to the bathroom. I heard crying and whimpering and the tiny voice of a four-year-old begging to be free of some horrible action. I began to shake on the toilet, not quite able to comprehend the true nature of my sister's moans and screams and seemingly painful experience. I could hear another voice exemplified by the repeated striking of an out-of-control woman. Was my sister being attacked by a monster from *The Twilight*

Zone, a television program that frightened me, or was a boogeyman or boogeywoman taking control of her? Mitzy was screaming and crying and begging and clearly in agony. I could hear skin to skin contact, and then Mitzy went silent.

I quickly thought of locking the bathroom door. Or would I or could I, as a six-year-old child, be capable of opening the one wooden window to cry for help? Who would I scream for? The land was a desolate former hog farm. Dirt roads led to the sites of future homes. We were situated down a hill and through the woods. No one lived near us, and so I was sure I was going to be knifed or burned or shot at like the hunters shooting the deer, and then I would die at the mercy of the monster who must have killed my sister.

I did nothing because I was frozen on the toilet, shaking with fear. I heard the "monster" pounding its feet on each of the thirteen wooden steps coming closer and closer to the second level where I was. I had no idea of my fate. Then the door flew open, and I viewed the rage of a red-faced, hundred-pound woman with a wooden spoon in her hand. Her veins were popping from her neck. She lunged toward me, dropping the spoon and literally lifting me off the toilet and beating me with all her might and physical strength with the slap of her hand. I saw the devil, and she had the anger of a damaging tornado. I saw a monster.

I cried out in hopeless pleas. "Stop, please stop. Don't kill me. Please, no please." It hurt. I lifted my arms to protect my back, my legs, my buttocks, and my face. I could not get free of the monster's grasp on my left arm. She held my head against the green tiled wall.

After several tumultuous minutes the monster stopped, cursed me, yelled at me, and left me on the cold ceramic floor to die. I was in pain. I was stunned. I was scared.

The monster was identifiable. The monster was my mother.

At that moment I realized that the image of a "mother" could switch to an image of a killer. I was confused and frightened, and I prayed that it never happened again. I also realized that I was not dead, all my body parts were intact, and that there was fresh urine on the floor. I had peed myself during the beating. I prayed I could wipe up the urine before she returned. I was too frightened to go back downstairs, but I heard the monster calling me.

"Tracey, come down here. Now! Right now!"

I walked down the stairs and into the kitchen, shaking with fright. Our mother was at the stove, calmly stirring a hollandaise sauce. Many bags of groceries were on the kitchen floor, and my sister Mitzy was sitting meekly and quietly on the kitchen table, looking thoroughly abashed and saying absolutely nothing. She was alive. Her deep blue eyes, which were so big and beautiful, looked sad. Our mother stood quietly at the stove, holding the handle of a Paul Revere copper-bottomed saucepan while reflecting on a Betty Crocker Cookbook in a red binder that lay open on the white and gold Formica countertop. She was wearing plaid shorts, which came to her knees; a sleeveless, well-starched and collared white blouse; and, as always, Daniel Green slippers that looked more like an outdoor sandal with a hard sole than a soft slipper. She wore no makeup except a hint of pink frosted lipstick. She had a nun like short hairstyle, a style too old for her age. She wore no jewelry except her platinum set, round diamond wedding and engagement rings. She had large white teeth that she clenched most of the time. As she stirred the hollandaise sauce, she demanded to know what Mitzy and I had done when she'd driven off to Giant Food, a local grocery store, to get groceries, leaving us, age four and age six, alone.

I began to explain the series of events. "Well, after you left, Mitzy and I ate our sandwiches. And we decided to make you happy and do a good job cleaning up our crumbs, so we went into the cabinet and used Ajax cleanser that you use to clean up our crumbs in the sink."

Mitzy and I had been eating Wonder Bread sandwiches, which consisted of peanut butter and marshmallow spread, when our mother had announced that she was going to Giant Food, approximately ten miles away. She'd instructed us to be good and to not open the door if someone rang the doorbell. She'd also warned us not to make a mess.

After we had eaten our sandwiches, the two of us had made a plan to use paper towels and really clean the table well, to please our mother. On many occasions, we'd witnessed our mother take out Ajax cleanser and scrub the stainless steel sink. The cleaner smelled refreshing, and the sink glistened when she scrubbed it. Our fateful error that day was applying the Ajax cleanser with our small hands and hearts onto a new Ethan Allen wood kitchen table. My sister and I thought we were being helpful. Our eager intent was to please our mother. As we wiped the cleanser into the wood, we noticed that the wood turned a bit white. We used more water on additional paper towels to bring the wood color back—to no avail.

As we'd waited for our mother to come home, we'd had no idea that our cleanup project would elicit such a violent response.

Even back then, I started referring to her as "our mother." She was no longer mine. Even at such a young age, my disconnect was complete. Although I was young, I did not want to umbrella myself under her "care" and "wisdom"—things that were reserved for true, warmer mothers. True mothers did not beat their children. True mothers disciplined and guided but did not bring their offspring to death's door.

Ever since that day, fifty-two years ago, I cannot bear to look at Ajax cleanser in the grocery store. As my mother lashed out at my tiny body, I could feel her round diamond wedding ring striking my skin. Every time I saw her hand rise up to deliver another slap filled with vitriol, I saw her ring. For a second during the attack, I wondered if her ring would fall off. I wanted it to fall off.

From that day forward, to forget the trauma to my body, I would lose myself in pleasant thoughts or in the words of a book, any book. With that, I became an instant daydreamer. I selected books with a positive theme and also learned to memorize things, like sign language, by staring at pictures in a book. I immersed myself in learning, dreaming, anything to prevent myself from dwelling on our home environment. Even today, I can remember things I read years ago. I did the same with movies. I concentrated on a movie to such a degree that I can remember the minutest detail. I tried hard to remove any beatings from my brain and force it to be occupied with more positive images or expressions. The beatings were so abnormal, and a peaceful normalcy was something I thrived to achieve throughout the rest of my life.

That day ended quietly. Our mother never mentioned this incident again. As my siblings came home, not a word was spoken. My father, unaware that two of his very small girls had been bludgeoned with such emotional rage and physical anger, was greeted at the kitchen door. He kissed Mitzy and me. We were relieved to see him at home, and then we simply went to bed.

Like the Ajax cleanser and the round diamond, the green bathroom would forever change. It would no longer be a place of daydreams, a place where I would stare out the window or into the mirror, hoping to grow up and be like one of the beautiful actresses on television. The bathroom was tainted by the memory of a fierce and harmful beating and its resulting damage, both tangible and intangible. It was there that I had witnessed a lunatic attack her children, and therefore, from that day forward, I never remained too long in the green bathroom. What amazed me was how strong our mother seemed to be. She had huge force and energy. I could only fathom how she'd found the strength to propel such rage at us.

WHEN I WOKE UP THE next day, I noticed bruises all over my arms and legs. Mitzy's arms and legs were worse, as she was thinner. Our mother told us to stay in our rooms because she was having company. She would alert us when we could come downstairs. The rule was very simple. She told us what to do, and we did it because she said so. Using fear, she made sure you heard her command once and only once. She did not repeat herself. We faced a beating if she was forced to repeat herself.

The front doorbell rang, and I heard a familiar and beloved voice. The voice belonged to one of my mother's friends, Kitty Carson. Kitty was a woman born before her time. While most women were stay-at-home mothers, Kitty's goal was to sell every house in our town and make a ton of money while doing it. She sold real estate for a gentleman named Hollis T. Brown, and she was proud of her accomplishments. Her for sale signs were everywhere, and she treated herself to expensive cars.

Upon her arrival, Kitty asked our mother where the children were, and our mother summoned us to come downstairs and say hello. It was great to see Kitty. She was soothing to the eye and a welcome person, who brought normalcy. Her presence ensured us that our mother would act more normal.

"Tracey, my sweet, how are you?" Kitty asked.

I embraced her, and she pulled me back to take a look at me. I had moaned a little from the pain of the embrace when she'd touched my bruises. The bruises were quite evident, and when Kitty saw them, a bit of confusion appeared on her face.

"What on earth happened to you?" Kitty demanded. "Where did you get all these bruises?" she asked as she touched my arm.

Our mother, listening to Kitty's questioning, clenched her teeth and immediately jumped in. "Tracey got the bruises during a baton lesson." Our mother glared at me with her fierce face. The face was a reminder to say nothing. We children learned never ever to cross our mother, especially when she gave us the fierce face look. Disobeying the face always meant paying the price—a healthy dose of verbal abuse and a good beating.

Throughout my life, Kitty remained a constant presence. When I received my First Communion, Kitty was there. When I graduated from every level of education, Kitty was there. When I dressed for my proms and homecoming events, Kitty was there. We dined together and laughed together and, at one point, even worked together.

Years later, after I had reached adulthood and escaped our mother's grasp, I would learn that Kitty often reflected on the abuse she knew was taking place in our home. She felt trapped and incapable of intervening. The women in our community would never dare cross our mother, she would explain. She was such a "pillar" in our small town that folks would look crazy for the smallest mention of abuse in our household. Kitty feared for us. She felt helpless because we were not her children. During one conversation after I graduated from college, while we were driving around in her blue Mercedes, Kitty broke down and cried.

"Tracey, I saw the bruises and felt your pain," she said. "I should have done more to get you and your siblings away from it."

CHAPTER TWO

---•---

THE TWO OF THEM

WHAT FORMS AN ABUSER IS often a mystery. How does a human being end up being so cold, so angry, so full of rage? Certainly, if you look into our mother's ancestry, the abusive tendencies did not come from my grandmother, who would walk around a small bug for fear of harming it. With complete bewilderment, my siblings and I often wondered how on earth our father, nicknamed "Buddy J" had fallen in love with such a monster. She must have kept her private personality from him as long as she could. If the real human being had been put on display, he would have run faster than his horses. We also wondered why, if she resented us so much, she continued to have more children.

To try to understand where the monster within came from, I delved into the events of our mother's life. Our mother and father were married on December 3, 1955, on a cold, wet day in a Catholic church outside Boston. My father's steeplechase father was too drunk to attend the wedding, but his estranged wife did attend. Our mother described my father's father as a drunk and described my father's mother as cold and distant. My paternal grandmother was a hairdresser and when our mother asked her if she would assist the bridesmaids with their hair on the wet wedding day, she replied, "No. This is my day off."

I presume this person was the only person on the planet who did not bow down and fulfill our mother's orders or demands. For some reason, knowing that another human being somehow said no to our mother gives me great joy. The fact that the hair incident bothered her for years gives me even more satisfaction.

My parents began their married lives traveling up and down the East Coast to various racetracks—Gulfstream, Hialeah, Delaware Park, Havre de Grace, Laurel, Pimlico and Garden State. Because apartments generally did not allow short-term leases, this nomadic group of race trackers, consisting of jockeys, agents, trainers, valets, and groomsmen, pulled their residential mobile homes and anchored them in areas outside the tracks for thirty- or sixty-day meets and then would move on with the precision of the Native Americans depicted in *Dancing with Wolves*. Our mother repeated many times that this time of her life was her happiest. Happy? She never ever seemed happy. That word was not a word to describe her or her temperament. So what went so wrong?

Nine months after my parents were married, their first child, Tricia Ann was born. And thirteen months after Tricia's birth, I was born. Mitzy came two years later. Our mother constantly noted that having the third child was like putting the nails in a coffin. During those early days, I cannot remember abuse per se toward me. But I remember that Tricia, at a very young age, would hold her breath until she blacked out, a type of spoiled temper tantrum, when she did not get her way. I remember my father picking her up and shaking her and screaming at her to breathe. Our parents were both quite concerned with the drama of their firstborn.

While visiting the pediatrician, our mother asked what to do about Tricia's temper tantrums. The pediatrician told her that, the next time Tricia threatened to or began to hold her breath, she should pick up a hairbrush and "beat her within an inch of her life." Seeing that our mother did, in fact, end up picking up the hairbrush and beating her toddler, I believe this instruction from the pediatrician was the future permission slip for our mother to hit and strike out at her frail babies. If they acted up, the cure was to strike them. If they bothered you, strike them. If they unnerved you, strike them. This was a perfect solution to keeping children under control. After the hairbrush remedy, Tricia never blacked out on her own accord again.

OUR MOTHER AND FATHER WERE Catholic, and with Catholicism in the 1950s, '60s, and '70s came staunch demands to forego birth control. Thus, my parents had seven children in nine years. Our mother mentioned that she had two menstrual cycles in nine years because she was always either pregnant or lactating. Maybe her rage was due to bipolar personality disorder? Or maybe her discontent was the result of postpartum depression? I rather thought it was from stupidity. She had too many babies and just could not handle it emotionally.

After Buddy, the first son, was born came Anna. That is when my parents decided to anchor into a community. The final two, Robby and "Baby Sister," would not be born until after the "big house"—the house with the green bathroom—was built. My parents interviewed builders and decided to contract with a builder who would construct a home in an area being developed by a local developer, horse lover, and politico. My parents selected a one-acre lot deep in the planned community. Later, my mother mentioned that she'd chosen the lot so no one would be able to hear her scream at us. This was a perfect setting for her. It was private and isolated. It was in the middle of the woods. She could jump up and down and beat her children and no one would see or hear anything.

CHAPTER THREE

SCHOOL: A REPRIEVAL

AS WE GREW UP, IT would come time to attend school. I imagined that we would receive a reprieve from our mother's beatings on school days, so I looked forward to my first day of school. One moment of visible warmth that I felt from our mother was on my first day of first grade. For some reason, I got extremely nervous as we were walking up to St. Mary's of the Mills School.

The school was managed by the Pallottine Sisters, comprised mostly of German nuns who'd left Germany as Adolph Hitler had come into power. Their strong accents, a bit frightening on that first day, would prove difficult for me. Their clothing was odd too. They wore dark habits that surrounded their bodies, with the exception of their faces. It looked pretty odd and pretty scary too. I recall our mother holding my hand. It is the only time in my memory bank that she ever held my hand.

Our mother knelt down beside me and brushed away my tears. "Don't let Sister Celine see you crying," she said. "Be brave. Your sister is in the building with you."

That was the last time our mother attempted to truly nurture me or exhibit to me any sign of compassion. Shamefully those tender seconds were the only tender seconds that I can recall.

Throughout my life, I thirsted to hear more kind words. At the passage of each new stage and life event, her voice was always silent unless to express disdain. We were little troopers facing a battlefield of insults and assaults. How we survived is as much a mystery as what biological makeup produced her strife against us.

The theme song would be the same throughout our lives. Don't let anyone see you crying. Don't let anyone see your room unkempt. Don't let anyone see your skin with pimples. Don't let anyone see a bad report card. Don't let anyone see you fail or get poor grades. Don't let anyone catch on that there is abuse in our home and where the bruises came from.

AT ST. MARY'S OF THE Mills Catholic School in the 1960s, strict discipline was as much a part of the program as was learning English and math. Corporal discipline was an acceptable practice. Our mother permitted the nuns to slap a hand, a face, and a buttocks. Uncontrolled boys tended to receive more discipline than the girls. Habitually, a young blond boy named Ricky got summoned up to the nun's desk. Once there, he'd be asked to lean over her lap, and he'd get five or six strikes on the bottom. His punishment was for the crime of squirming in his seat or giggling at some funny moment. Watching Ricky get whipped reminded me of watching my own two brothers. Ricky resembled them. To this day, I mentally reach out to him, hoping that he too is well.

Our first grade class consisted of sixty-eight children in one room. Hygiene was an issue, so we routinely lined up for a head lice examination by Sister Celine. She also despised the habit of chewing fingernails. My best friend, Margaret, chewed her nails down to the skin, so when Sister Celine demanded that each of us place our hands on our desk while she inspected our small fingers, I feared for Margaret.

One day, Sister Celine walked slowly around the room with a wide ruler, and when she saw that you were a nail chewer, she slammed the ruler down on your hands. Margaret began to cry as she watched the children take their punishment. Her mother would apply an orange, ill-tasting liquid to her nails to prevent her from the habit, but Margaret would chew them anyway. When Sister Celine came upon Margaret, Margaret received ten strikes. Sister Celine said that each strike was for each finger that Margaret chewed. Then Sister Celine turned to me. With my hands stretched on the desk, I knew I was free because I did not chew my nails. Sister Celine struck down twice upon my hands, and I was taken aback.

I blurted out, "I don't chew my nails. My mother cuts my nails with scissors."

Sister Celine turned around and slapped me across the face for talking disrespectfully at her.

I had blurted out the statement. It was a simple, honest, excited utterance. The nun, like the pediatrician, and like our mother, struck out or recommended striking out, in order to ensure compliance.

Yet, the physical assaults from the nuns were pretty much forgiven; they, after all, were not labeled "mother." They were strangers who did not sleep close to us, who did not eat with us, who did not visit relatives with us. Mothers were supposed to be the full embodiment of warmth and love. The nuns were not deemed to be in that role. They were the educators, no matter how hard they had to drill the lessons we were to learn into our heads. We never received excessive cruelty of treatment from them. That was reserved for the closer person, our mother.

Chapter Four

Uncle Carl and the Beatles

When we moved into the big house in 1962, Anna, the fifth child, was a baby. We called her the Easter baby because she was born on Easter. She had a round face and big, circular eyes and was about as cute as a button. We created a rhyme for her: "Anna banana with the meatball eyes. You put her in the oven, and you get French fries." She howled every time we recited it.

My parents were enthusiastic about their new home, and our mother invited my uncle, her brother Carl, to visit. Carl was the last child of my grandmother's second marriage, and he was just a teenager when he came to see the big house. Our mother repeatedly told us that, when she graduated from nursing school, she had felt embarrassed that her own mother was very pregnant with Carl. Nonetheless, Carl was born and immediately evidenced musical talent. He enjoyed the latest hits and loved to be around us since we adored him.

Carl arrived at the airport just like his mother would do on occasion. Like her, he carried treats with him. He was also carrying a record player, a record holder canister, and a tape recorder. He was overjoyed to play us his records featuring a very popular new singing group called the Beatles. Upon arriving at our home, Carl immediately located a nice spot in the family room to plug in his latest equipment. Our mother was preparing a meal in the kitchen, and she seemed happy to see Carl. Tricia, myself, Mitzy, Buddy, and little Anna surrounded our beloved uncle, who was close to our age. He was more like an older brother than an uncle.

We were anticipating the playing of a song called "Help!" Carl patiently showed us his 45 rpm record with the picture of the Beatles, and we immediately chuckled at the sight of their hair. Carl showed us small baseball type cards or trading cards with pictures of all the Beatles and gave us some. Like baseball cards, these cards also came in small packs of bubble gum. We were intrigued by the way the "Fab Four" looked.

Carl was so impressed with his record player that he made sure we took very good care of it. He showed us the needle to the record player and showed us how to avoid scratching the record. He gently assembled the box of records, allowing us to look at the record covers. He told us to sit down and listen. Then he turned the record player on, and for some reason, we began to dance about the family room. We were so happy. We were happy to be with our uncle, and we were happy to see this new device, the record player.

Anna, the baby, not yet one year of age, was too young to stand up, so she was sitting and clapping her hands and just smiling at us. She sat next to the brick fireplace. Her hair was thin and blond. She wore her white, polished baby shoes and a simple, cotton dress. I think she was attempting to sing along: "Help, I need somebody / Help not just anybody."

Then something caught my attention, and I turned to see our mother—not with a smile on her face or a skip in her heart. No, the fierce, tooth-clenching, red-faced, angry monster had entered the room. She ran across the rug but could not immediately get hold of any of the older children. We were in motion, first dancing and now running, and although she lunged, she could not grab us. So she took hold of Anna, the baby, and pulled her by her baby hair and shook her while her little feet dangled, and then she dropped her onto the floor. Anna's face turned bright red. She attempted to crawl away, like a puppy retreating from its abusive owner. Throughout the attack, our mother was screaming, "Stop this noise. Stop this noise."

Carl picked Anna up and soothed her. Carl looked at his sister, "It was my fault," he said. "I made the noise. It was me."

Our mother stepped over the record player and yanked the chord out of the electrical socket. She kicked the record player and screamed, "Dinner is ready. Turn that damn thing off and come to dinner."

The words to the song were appropriate: "Help, I need somebody."

Our mother seldom lashed out at us with anyone else in her presence. It frightened me that she'd committed such an assault in the presence of my uncle. This meant she was opening the door to a wider audience, and the possibility that we were not exempt from her lashings while in the presence of others now loomed. After baby Anna was victimized, I knew that a whole new realm of beatings was possible. Now Carl had witnessed the event, which meant she could easily repeat it. Maybe she did not care, since Carl lived so far away. Her community reputation would remain intact; she knew her brother would not comment on what he'd witnessed within the community, and thus, her reputation would be spared.

Until Anna was five years old, she had trouble speaking. At one point, our mother took her to an audiologist thinking she was deaf. I always thought Anna's arrested development was because our mother shook her so hard that she lapsed into silence.

Uncle Carl was a gentle soul. For some reason he never moved far from his hometown of Salem, New Hampshire. He never married or had children. I often wondered how he earned a living. He strummed his guitar constantly, hoping to create a musical career. His band was good but never made the income to sustain itself. Carl drank a lot, and unfortunately, the drinking cost him his liver. When Carl died, I thought about how unbalanced the world is. His gentle spirit was buried in the coffin with him, yet our mother's hostility lived on. I guess such is the balance of good and evil.

Seeing baby Anna hurt was awful. It was not a relief to have any of my sisters or brothers beaten instead of me. In fact, it was quite the opposite; the visual images of my siblings' beatings were impregnated in my brain with no chance of escape. Today, I often wish for a cleansing for my brain's "hard drive"; then the memories would not float upon me and lace their sadness over the excitement of a sweeter life.

As a victim of familial abuse, you learn to hide the trauma, to avoid the stigma of being a victim. You do not want "it" to enter the room before you do. You want to excel and to achieve and to be popular. You want the outside depiction of the family life to be accurate, if not in reality, at least in other people's minds. Visitors left our home happy. I never wanted anyone to catch on, for fear of blemishing the family name or changing people's opinion of me. You learn to prevent the stigmatization of being abused by hiding it just as much as the perpetrator does. In essence, I became very much like our mother. I hid the abuse and got good at hiding it.

As a child, I felt that no one would believe me or my siblings if we were to tell someone about the abuse anyway. Surely, we would be called out as deserving of such reprimand and judged accordingly. We knew that adults would ask, "What did you do to upset your mother?" They saw her as a respectable human being. Surely, we would be labeled the culprits who'd upset such a stellar human. If only they knew that a simple thing like laughing to the Beatles ignited a firestorm.

CHAPTER FIVE

———————◆———————

PERFECTION AND CONTROL

THE TIMES WERE DIFFERENT IN the 1950s, '60s, and '70s. Women popularized the expression "stay-at-home mom" and created social lives, with admittance into bridge clubs, book clubs, women's clubs, and other similar groups. For our mother, those clubs were a reprieve from the doldrums of cooking, cleaning, and laundry. Our mother made sure the members of those clubs thought she was nothing less than extraordinary. She created a reputation for being exemplary and successfully hid her true persona from the public. I knew she had two distinct personalities residing in two completely different worlds. Her public persona, complete with volunteering and charity work, was admired and looked upon by many with awe. Her private persona was a deeply resentful woman who lashed out with physical and verbal abuse at the constant interruptions of her active children.

Our mother was a housekeeping perfectionist. She was not going to allow five children under the age of seven to modify her depiction, perception, and pronouncement of perfection. Our mother gave us chores to do early on, and we became a bit fanatical like her.

We resided on a one-acre lot, so work was needed on the exterior as well as the interior. Mitzy and Buddy were ascribed the outdoor chores, and Tricia and myself were deemed the inside cleaners. So with dust cloths in hand, Tricia and I dusted the entire house, utilizing chairs to reach the areas too tall for our short arms. One jockey's wife was aghast when she came to visit and witnessed our mother cleaning the corners of the house with Q-tips and single-handedly moving the furniture to retrieve a dust ball. When this woman looked over at the children cleaning on their hands and knees, she simply shook her head.

Knowing every clean inch of the home from top to bottom due to never-ending cleaning, Mitzy and I were surprised to one day discover bats in the attic. We shared one of the four bedrooms on the second level. Lying in our twin beds at night, we could hear crying and moaning, which we thought was outside our window. Every night, we would listen and surmised that cats were crying below. Now and then, when the cries got more pronounced, we would walk to our mother's bedroom with concern. Repeatedly, her response was "Get back to your Goddamn bed and go to sleep."

My father had become pretty immune to her verbal assaults. He learned to just shut it out or, better yet, stay at work as long as he could to avoid the nastiness. If home, he retreated to his basement workshop to avoid confrontation with her. Robby would sometimes say to me that he felt that our father was a squid, lacking a backbone, so to speak. I just think he was such a gentle soul that he did not want to antagonize her. Nonetheless, he stayed out of the line of fire for the most part.

One day, our mother ordered Mitzy to bring two large lamps to the attic and place them against the far wall. Without hesitation, Mitzy yanked on the attic rope, pulled the folded steps down, and walked up to pull the string to the light bulb to illuminate her way. I could hear her footsteps walking across the planks and then, all of a sudden, I heard her scream and run back and literally jump past the steps and hurl the panel back to the ceiling. Our mother came running, hit Mitzy for screaming, and demanded to know why she was making such a commotion.

"There are things hanging on the wall," said Mitzy, "like little monsters."

Our mother continued to strike Mitzy, screaming, "There are no such things as monsters."

Doubting Mitzy yet observing how fearful Mitzy was, our mother pulled the attic steps down, walked up, and marched to the wall. She then screamed. I wanted to push the steps back up to the ceiling and trap her in there so the monsters could eat her, but she was too fast. She folded up the steps and ran to our neighbor, a local hardware store owner.

Upon inspection, seventy-eight bats were found in our attic. The little moans and cries that Mitzy and I'd been hearing all night were actually bats.

Nonetheless, cleaning was to continue, bats or no bats. And Mitzy got beaten for discovering the bats, as if she'd placed them there.

Our home included the best cleaning tools and the best scrubbing products. We had a huge, heavy, stand-up Kirby vacuum cleaner. One day, as usual, our mother demanded that I start vacuuming the carpet, which had recently been placed over our wooden flooring. I was also to vacuum every step leading to the second floor. I decided, in an effort to please this woman, to work diligently on the steps, moving the hose attachment in a horizontal motion. The lines looked sharp and clean and evenly spaced. I was proud of my job. It took a long time to remove every dust particle on every step.

Our mother came around the corner where I was admiring my effort; all of a sudden, my hair was being pulled out of my scalp. My head was yanked, and I felt the swing of her skinny arm striking across my body. She thrust my head against the wall and looked at me while grinding her teeth. Our mother was not happy.

As I cried and moaned and tried to pull away she snarled, "Do those Goddamn stairs again, and this time, use vertical strokes, you idiot."

I carried the heavy vacuum up the thirteen steps and proceeded to vacuum the stairs in a vertical stroke.

Just then, the front doorbell rang, and Kitty walked into the foyer announcing her presence. When she looked up the stairs and saw me, she said, "Tracey Mary, why are you holding something ten times bigger than you? You are going to fall down those stairs. Come down from the stairs." Immediately, she ran up the steps and grabbed the vacuum from my hands.

Our mother came around the corner, aware of Kitty's entrance into our home, and said, "Kitty, do not disrupt Tracey's chores."

Kitty turned to her and said, "She is going to kill herself with that heavy vacuum. She is too small for this job."

Our mother ignored her statements. "Tracey, keep working and do it right," she ordered.

She barked the orders, and like obedient little soldiers, we did what she demanded. Even with Kitty there, this moment was no exception.

With visitors, our mother took pride in showing off her clean and beautiful house. Our mother made a point of opening up the linen closets to show off her firmly pressed sheets and pillow cases.

The only way we could get a reprieve from her anger was to avoid being in the same room as her by distancing us from her. If she was on the first floor, we tried to position ourselves on the second floor. Our chores were to be performed to perfection. Without perfection, punishment would ensue, and this frightened us. If she asked us to sweep the garage, and upon inspection, the garage was still riddled with leaves, she would terrorize us with fits of rage and violent temper tantrums.

Upon outdoor inspections, our mother could be heard screaming at Buddy and Mitzy, "Broom sweep these patios and get all the goddamn grass off them."

Seldom did she attack Mitzy. Mitzy was deemed different. She was not as mentally fast as the rest of us children were. She was not assertive or demonstrative, so our mother had her tested at the recommendation of our pediatrician. Mitzy was not mentally disabled, but our pediatrician did not like some of the results of the mental acuity testing he did on her. After some rigorous testing, Mitzy was labeled "different."

This conclusion always seemed a bit unfair. In truth, the other children in the family were extroverts, and Mitzy simply appeared to be an introvert, a quiet soul. When people met Mitzy, they always questioned whether she was biologically related to us. All my siblings were extroverts and were not shy by any means. We were comfortable around classmates, teachers, and neighbors. Mitzy was not. We knew it throughout our childhood. Even today she is an introvert and pretty much stays to herself. During discussions between our mother and the pediatrician, the pediatrician somehow got our mother to acknowledge that Mitzy should be treated with "gentler" hands. Thus, although Mitzy had been beaten the day of the Ajax cleanser incident, her subsequent diagnosis gave her a bit of a hall pass. The physical beatings Mitzy received were not as severe as those dealt out to the rest of us. She continued to get hit but not as hard.

THE STRICTURES OF PARENTING IN that era resembled a Victorian way of bringing up children. Corporal punishment intended to cause physical punishment, pain, and chastisement was common. Spanking, paddling, or caning by parents, guardians, school officials, and other authority figures was an accepted practice and is, as of this writing, still a common practice in many states.

Our mother must have read the book on the theory because she practiced it almost hourly. She would deliberately inflict physical pain in response to some undesired behavior. Unfortunately, her tolerance level meant that, to her, normal childhood conduct fit the category of undesired behavior. Every slap or pinch was an anecdote for her resentment toward us.

I was not certain if my friends experienced the same type of parenting that my siblings and I experienced during our childhoods. I never witnessed any beatings while visiting friends; nor did I observe any unusual bruises.

Our mother's insistence on maintaining a spotless home often left me feeling uncomfortable and many times a bit of a failure for not living up to her expectations of cleanliness. I was never completely relaxed, for fear of making a mess. I never felt that our mother would protect me from anything except dust.

Save for the hand holding moment in the first grade, only one instance of our mother offering protection stands out in my mind.

I adored a dark haired girl named Lydia and would spend the night at her home, which was a rented apartment, quite often. Lydia was the only child I knew with divorced parents. Additionally, she was the only friend who sprung into puberty sooner than any of the rest of us. Lydia would always ask me if my period had come just so we could compare the experience. Repeatedly, I told her no, and for the next several years, my answer remained no. Her mother was a stunning beauty who fell in love with a burly looking man and married him. He seemed pleasant and hard-working and gave me no reason to fear him until early one morning.

Unlike our family, Lydia's family did not attend Sunday morning church services, even though Lydia attended Catholic school with us. It was fun to skip church and to just linger in bed and laugh with her. Typically, we would wake up very tired because we would talk all evening.

One morning, her stepfather bolted through the door demanding that Lydia wake up. Lydia did not move. Her stepfather then approached her, removed the sheet from her, flipped her from her back to her stomach, pulled her pants down, and moved his hand around her pelvic area. Lydia still did not move. Then he flipped the sheet over her and left. I pretended to be asleep.

When I got out of bed, I asked Lydia if I could call our mother. I asked our mother to immediately come pick me up. Hearing the sound of my voice, she came quickly. While driving home in the car, I told her what had happened. For the only time in my life, she decided to protect me and never allowed me to visit Lydia at the apartment again. Our mother also made sure that Lydia's stepfather never came close to me.

Chapter Six

NOT LIKE HER MOTHER

I OFTEN WONDERED HOW OUR mother became the type of person she was. I was, and still am, bewildered by the composition of her, or any other abuser for that matter, and the layers of life that create such a person. I saw none of our mother's traits in my grandmother, Rita. My grandmother was the complete opposite of our mother. She was demonstrative and vibrant, and she laughed and smiled all the time. She wore high knee boots and held a small dog in a large pocketbook and drove a Mustang with the license plate "LIBRA" on it. She smelled like a beautiful lotion, and I always loved it when she lay besides me in bed because her scent lingered past her presence. My grandmother's presence was an oasis of joy. I always felt protected next to her. She, in time, became totally unaware of the daily mistreatment of her grandchildren.

My grandmother was a French woman but a proud New Englander. She provided for her family by cooking at a German restaurant, managing a local golf course, and occasionally cooking for the parish priests. She had devoted, fun friends who met once a month in her home, closed the door to the parlor, and laughed for the duration of the evening. Those gatherings were secretive, closed sessions, and the discussions were as private as an AA meeting. Years later, I discovered that one of the group "members" carried on an affair with a priest for thirty years. Additionally, when the sons of the members were drafted to fight in the Vietnam War and came home smoking pot, the parlor club took it upon themselves to roll a few joints and get high. My grandmother's address was 22 Happy Street, a fitting name for a warm woman, and the welcome mat to many.

My grandmother would fly in to visit us. Anxiously, my siblings and I would peer through the windows of the airport to watch the plane drop off our energetic, beautiful grandmother. She always prepared food and brought it with her—as much as she could carry. Her bags would be filled with lobster pie, cream puffs, and fudge. Within her luggage were her little flasks of brandy and gin, mink stoles, and lovely perfumes. Upon seeing us, she would greet us with her trademark greeting, "Darlings!" She would sweep each of us up in her arms, and I could smell that dreamy perfume and lotion and see the beautiful face of a sweet and vivacious woman. Unlike our mother's bitter smell of Clorox, my grandmother depicted sexuality and epitomized femininity and fun. She could make a grand entrance into the soul of everyone. To succumb to my grandmother's presence meant that one would behold what she admired most—a beautiful flower, the art of a handcrafted railing, the significance of a delicately painted portrait. She breathed in life, joy, and optimism. She was a refreshing wind coming through our home, and I wanted her to visit all the time.

Rita loved bath time. She would place Tricia, myself, and Mitzy into the tub, fill it with bubble bath, and belt out the words to the song "Lemon Tree." I can still close my eyes and hear her singing, "Lemon Tree, very pretty and the lemon flower is sweet but the fruit of the poor lemon is impossible to eat." We would cheer and giggle when she sang it.

During one certain bath, my grandmother asked us repeatedly how we had gotten so many bruises on our arms, legs, backs, and shoulders.

She finally asked, "Who did this to you?"

I cannot remember who blurted it out, but one of my sisters said, "Mommy."

She dried each one of us tenderly with a soft towel and a warm touch. Then she marched downstairs to the kitchen, and demanded to know from our mother how the bruises had gotten on our bodies. I heard my grandmother say to our mother, "I think you are abusing your children."

Our mother's response was icy and final. "Pack your bags," she said, her eyes cold. "I will be taking you to the airport in the morning."

As soon as the sun came up, I heard commotion in the house. My grandmother was begging our mother to be reasonable. Our mother stood her ground. She was not to be scolded, reprimanded, or criticized. I heard her say, "This is my house, and I will do whatever I want in my house."

We sat with our faces against the window of the airport and watched our lovely grandmother fly off back to New England.

NOW OUR MOTHER WAS ALONE, free to strike her children without any interference and away from the judgmental eyes of our lovely, well-intended grandmother. As an abuser, our mother sheltered herself inside a cocoon of isolation so that witnesses were few, if any. Our mother had a lifetime habit of cutting people out of her life who dared to criticize her or sympathize with us children. She would close the door on them just as easily as she closed the door to our home in the woods.

Years later, while riding the Metro Rail in Washington, DC, with my grandmother, I asked her about that moment.

31

"I don't know where your mother came from …" she said, her voice trailing off. "Maybe her father, Ira Levenstein. He was sharp-spirited like your mother. That is why we divorced. He put his hands on me one too many times, and I had enough. Your mother reminds me of him. The two of them are mean and angry. Your mother was so brutal towards you children. But unfortunately I learned not to speak up."

"Why?" I asked. "Why did you not speak up?"

She said, "Because on that day, after your mom brought me to the airport, she did not speak to me for one year. And I wanted to be part of your lives."

At five foot two and one hundred pounds, our mother had a lot of power and weight. She ruled. Even her own mother learned not to cross her.

Abusers come in all packages and from all socioeconomic classes. Who would have thought that Heisman trophy winner O. J. Simpson had such a temper toward his loved one? Who would think that Marilyn Van Derbur, a 1958 Miss America winner from a very respected family, was being sexually abused by her father? Abusers do not necessarily look like creepy men with hatchets. They are the men and women who go to church, who volunteer at functions, who run for president of the PTA. They can be educated or high school dropouts. There is no particular physical trait that enables you to pick them out in a crowd. But one thing is certain. They are sick and in need of immediate counseling or censure for that matter.

Chapter Seven

———◆———

Clean Drawers, a Wooded Field, and the Reservoir

THERE WERE DAILY HABITS IN our household. As the alarm clock began to ring, our mother would start her day with a scream. "Time to get your lazy asses up." That is how we were greeted. If we did not immediately jump from our beds, she would pull us out of bed with a strike of the hand or a pull of the hair. You could always feel the diamond ring pierce your flesh. On school days, she screamed her lungs out until the last of us, with our black Labrador retriever at our side, were out the door for the walk to the school bus stop. For the next seven hours, she was alone in her house, cleaning incessantly.

There were also habits that were infrequent and perhaps even more frightening because of the predictable unpredictability. On several occasions, we would arrive home from school, sweaty and tired, and see our mother ironing clothes in the kitchen. Instantly, we could feel intense heat, and it was not from the iron. We were never greeted with, "How was your day?"

While clenching her teeth, she would say, "All of you go to your rooms and put your things back together correctly and organize your belongings."

We would walk up the steps slowly, knowing that we would see something tumultuous.

And there it would be. As we would move to our respective rooms, we would see the rage—sheer unadulterated rage. Several times a year, our mother would wait for us to leave for school and then enter each bedroom and pull everything out of every closet, drawer, or box. She would grab the toys, the clothes, the belts, the shoes, and the trinkets and dump all of it in the middle of the room. Then she would take everything off our desks and shelves and throw those items on top of the wreckage in the middle. She would proceed to empty every drawer, throwing whatever they contained on the heap and then literally toss the empty drawers on the floor. She was so obsessed with organization and cleanliness that she could not control herself when she began her rampage.

We would stand there for a moment, staring at our individual heaps. And then we would begin to put everything back into place.

As we replaced our items, our mother would be screaming around us, "Do it right! Throw away what you do not need and get it done before dinner."

It typically took three hours to deconstruct our mother's violent production of disarray and put our things back together. But we succeeded in making our rooms perfect and looked for approval that was never forthcoming.

The day following one of those "cleanouts" brought a simple joy. We walked to the school bus, our loyal Labrador by our side. The day was beautiful, and the air felt good. The other neighborhood children—the Paynes, the Melbournes, and the Delps—were also in good moods. But something was amiss.

Our youngest sibling, Baby Sister, was not among us. "Where's Baby?" became the anthem.

We were half a mile away from our home. We remembered that she'd left the house with us. Where had she gone?

As the bus approached our stop, we looked down toward our home and saw our blue station wagon with the wood panels approaching at a high rate of speed. Our mother was still in her pajamas. She jumped out of the car, moved toward us with teeth clenching and veins popping out of her neck, and yanked Baby out of the car. Baby was crying and had flushed cheeks. In front of the entire group of children on the bus, as well as those who walked to the bus stop with us, our mother removed one of her hard slippers and beat Baby for hiding in the garage and not walking to the bus stop. Our mother saw Baby as a noncompliant child and must have heard that pediatrician's voice: "Beat her within an inch of her life."

Baby, crying, entered the bus. We were beyond humiliated. We were mortified. As we sat stunned in our bus seats, one of the neighborhood children looked over and said, "Your mother is the meanest mother in the neighborhood."

Meanest mother in the neighborhood! What a title. I dreamed of a different title—happiest mother in the neighborhood or best cook in the neighborhood, not meanest mother in the neighborhood. The humiliation was unbearable. All seven of us were on the bus, and we were like stones. The other children stared at us as if we had some dreaded disease. We did not have the disease; our mother did. We were just not sure how far the disease would progress, how bad her abuse of us would get.

———————

IT WAS AT THIS TIME that I began to exercise more progressive coping mechanisms. I started to daydream in order to rid my brain of the events of my real life. Additionally, I perfected a happy-go-lucky face to hide the sadness. I also began to outpace everyone. I outpaced them with good grades, with my work ethic, by winning awards, and by volunteering for every possible activity. I became "Gidget gone busy" in order to run faster than the harmful thoughts. I leaned ahead and not back. If I sat too long, it would force me to think about our home life, and I surely would have sunk into a deep pit that I could not return from. I became a life runner in order to cope. Being a life runner prevented me from absorbing. There were too many activities and too much to achieve while sprinting ahead.

The abuse tarnished the overall beauty of our lovely street and the natural beauty of our neighborhood. In its infancy, our development was completely wooded. Birds, fox, deer, groundhogs, and just about every type of small animal lived among us. Since the area was so rural, we relied on well water for our water supply. The developer had a vision that, with the addition of more families, we would eventually hook up to the pipes of the Washington Suburban Sanitation Commission, a public water source.

We routinely played in the woods of this undeveloped parcel. We collected old bottles or a shiny rock or an unusual tree branch. We got poison ivy constantly. On a particular Saturday morning, Buddy wanted to make a trail in the woods to find a treasure, so I took him by the hand, and we began walking, smiling, talking, and imagining. I was seven years old, and he was four. Buddy was a cute little boy with a blond crew cut, large lips, and a broad nose that made all of us question our pure white heritage. He was a fun little boy with a nice personality. He loved to walk in the woods.

As we were frolicking in the woods, all of a sudden, the ground beneath Buddy caved in, and he fell down a long, narrow hole. I could barely see him. Frightened, he began to cry, and I could see him down the dark hole. He was reaching his arms toward me. I saw water around his feet and ankles. I leaned down to retrieve him but could not reach him and told him I was going to get our mother. He was terribly upset and did not want me to leave him.

I was terrified as I ran to the house through the sticker bushes, branches, and bugs. I ran up the driveway screaming that Buddy had fallen in a hole. Our mother came out with her wooden spoon and frantically hit me several times with it before demanding that I lead her to him. I pointed toward our play area.

She kept screaming, "You were supposed to watch your little brother. Why did you not watch your brother?"

As we ran, she continued to hit me. I got disoriented in the woods, but fortunately we could hear Buddy's moans and were able to locate him and reassure him we would pull him out.

Upon seeing how far down Buddy was, our mother ran back to the house to retrieve a thin, metal ladder. I could see fear on her face for the first time. It was comforting to see her frantic face. I did not see the normal expression she wore, which seemed to say, "I wish you were all dead." It appeared to me that she was quite concerned about Buddy's life.

For the next week, our mother treated me as if I had drilled the hole into the earth myself and sucked Buddy into it. Every time she repeated the story, she made sure to slap me.

As BUDDY GOT OLDER, HE got more mischievous and curious. At age three, my father bought him a hammer, and he proceeded to hammer every piece of furniture on the first floor. At age four, he lined the couch cushions up and leaned several glass coke bottles against them and decided to throw a small bowling ball against them. At age eight, he found a small firecracker, lit it on fire, and threw it onto the patio. Our Labrador retriever chased it, and it exploded in his mouth knocking several of the dog's teeth out. Buddy routinely strolled up to the Melbourne farm and released the horses from the paddocks. He would get beaten after each event or occurrence. Over time, his cute little smile and personality changed. He just molded into one of the older siblings. Fear became part of his complexion, and sadness laced his eyes.

In our rural area we were constantly in the woods playing, which made our mother happy. We were out of the house, and she could obsessively clean without us tumbling underfoot. She purchased and had installed a huge black bell attached to a rope on a tall pole. She would use it whenever she wanted us home. She would step outside the kitchen onto a patio and sidewalk lined with bug-ridden rose bushes and ring the bell. It was imperative that, whatever we were doing—jumping on the Delps' trampoline, riding our bikes, or walking in the woods—we ran home immediately.

On one particular day, our mother rang the bell and all of us came home except Buddy.

Our mother's "patience" ended when Buddy decided to ride his bike up to the reservoir and fish. He had been warned by her about a million times not to go to the reservoir, but he went in blatant defiance of her orders. To gain access to this body of water, Buddy had to ride his bike half a mile out of our neighborhood onto a more trafficked road, travel another mile, and then turn left onto a narrow strip called Supplee Lane, along which he would ride down to a desolate, wooded area. Of course, she was correct in her concerns, and warnings were warranted. A young boy alone near any type of water, especially in a desolate area, is dangerous to say the least. The terms *predator* and *pedophile* were not popular at the time, but water accidents and death were definitely fears.

Buddy disobeyed her stern warnings, grabbed his bike, rode out of the curvy street of our neighborhood onto the traffic of Brooklyn Bridge Road, and hung a left onto Supplee Lane. Immediately, out of nowhere, he was hit by a moving vehicle. Someone called an ambulance, and an attendant called our mother.

She exploded upon picking up the phone. She looked over at us and screamed at the top of her lungs that we were to sit still in the family room and not move a muscle. She angrily told us how much she hated us. We had no idea what had happened. She turned to us with her eyes bulging out of her head, clenching her teeth and yelled, "I am going to kill your fucking brother Buddy."

Our fucking brother Buddy. I had never heard that word *fucking*. It did not sound good. It did not sound nice. It sounded like a curse word. I aligned the word with *shit*. Our mother used that word all the time. Routinely, at dinnertime, we would ask our mother, "What's for dinner?"

Her typical response was "Shit on toast."

The expression made me sick, and it surely did not hone anyone's appetite. For years, I visualized our mother serving seven children and one unlucky husband plates of shit on toast.

Our mother arrived on Supplee Lane to find an ambulance with one male rescuer and two females; one broken, crooked bike; and a man who was frantically upset about having hit a young boy on his two-wheeler. My brother was lying on a stretcher. Upon seeing this milieu, our mother put a fist in the air and, leaning towards Buddy, said, "If you could stand up, I would knock you down."

How dare my brother disobey her and produce a scene of such imperfect mothering? Here was a boy lying on the ground with a bag of fish hooks, a fishing pole, bread and peanut butter for bait, and a broken bike and all of this quite distant from the main curtilage. She was not concerned for the health of her child but for the image of perfection—namely, the clean, neat, manner-driven children she wanted us to be. She lashed out at him and lunged at him to strike him. The ambulance driver shielded Buddy.

This was around 1970, and calls to social services were not as common as they are today. Calls placed against white Catholic women with a history of volunteering at the Catholic grade school, who were also Sunday school teachers, were especially rare and, when said woman was married to a revered local athlete, nearly unthinkable.

One of the female ambulance attendants witnessed and heard our mother and her anger and filed a report to social services for child abuse. Her report became more urgent when she learned that six other children were residing with this hostile woman.

In learning of the report, our mother was appalled that someone would dare question her and her manner in rearing children. Like she told my grandmother years before, "No one is going to tell me what to do in my house."

To prepare for the visit of the social services agents, our mother wet my and my sisters' hair and curled our hair with bobby pins, washed our prettiest clothes, and made us dust our rooms. Anticipating the visit, she warned us not to speak up, not to discuss anything, and to let her do the talking. She reminded us that we would be punished if we said anything.

Two individuals, one male and one female, came to the house and sat down with all of us in our wood-paneled family room. Our mother put on a good show. She became the epitome of perfection. Brownies on the counter. A pot roast in the oven. A well-stocked refrigerator and a home so neat and tidy that the linen closet boasted crisp, freshly ironed sheets and pillowcases.

The visit was short. I think the individuals were in awe of her, not critical of her. They left our home shaking her hand as if to say, "Job well done."

I felt disappointed. I had expected them to somehow save us. I'd expected them to interview us separately and possibly take us away. I'd expected them to possibly take *her* away.

When they departed, our mother turned off the charm, shut the door, and looked at us and said, "Motherfuckers can stay out of my house. How dare they!" She was truly smug. She'd fooled them and glossed over their concerns with her "good" personality. She could tolerate no criticism. Nor would she make improvements based on any suggestions. She would have made a paper airplane out of any written report or evaluation. It was her way or no way. She undoubtedly thought she had failed at the hiding of the abuse. At the fishing location where Buddy had been hit by the car, she'd let her anger take over, and the thing she most wanted to keep private—her treatment of her children had been exposed. If anything, she returned home to improve on the veil of secrecy, rather than the veil of loving her children.

She was smart during the week prior to the visit from social services. She did not hit us. And therefore, no fresh bruises would be evident on our skinny bodies. I think if our mother could have located the ambulance driver who'd initiated the report against her, she would have beaten her to death. And Buddy never rode his bike to the reservoir again.

I know it is difficult for a stranger to make assumptions when abuse is occurring in a home and to report the offenses. It is a big leap for the person with a good antenna to speak up. But it is imperative to make the call. When you see an abuse "flame," there is usually more fire than the small flame you witnessed. Most human beings can decipher right conduct and reasonable conduct in weighing a situation. Making the call shows strength, and it might just save a life or lives from a tumultuous situation. Day care providers, teachers, and doctors are all in a position to determine if a child or children are in need of assistance. They see the children and can compare the children's physical appearance and manner with those of multitudes of children. It does not take much to see one stand out in the crowd, and it is so crucial to inquire.

Chapter Eight

---◆---

Sunday Madness

OUR MOTHER FELT TRAPPED BY her seven children. She was a bright woman with immense organizational skills. Her biggest asset was a boundless amount of energy. She could conquer multitudes of chores and duties every day. With her large family, those skills were only evident in her community activities and home responsibilities, not in a career. Nonetheless, despite how deeply unfulfilled she was, she was not going to accept a paying job. I think she felt that a paying job would indicate that her husband was not capable of providing for the family, and she was not going to allow her friends to think that. Therefore, she volunteered at our Catholic school, where all seven of her children attended. I always felt it was another way for her to continue to control our every move and to stay in good standing with the community of teachers and priests. With her presence, we could never divulge what was happening at home to a teacher or person of authority. Given that she appeared as such a doer of good, how would, how could anyone label her an abuser? She was so good at the veil of secrecy that if I had been on the outside, I wouldn't have noticed anything either.

She resented us for her position in life. She chose it, but somehow blamed us for her choice.

Another escape from the beatings, besides the hours at school, was when our father would invite all the track "loners" to our home. I think he too knew that if a stranger was brought to the house, the verbal abuse that our mother directed toward him would not occur. With the various agents, jockeys, and trainers coming in and out of our home, our mother's attention was diverted to the roll of "hostess with the mostest" and not "batterer."

By the end of the week, we would be exhausted. The weekends were not pleasurable because we were confined to her presence and demands. With the weekends came two things—directives and slaps from her. We just had to get through Sundays, and then the school days would deliver us from evil.

Every Sunday was a nightmare in our home. Trying to get seven children clean and sparkling and out the door to attend Mass was difficult. Our mother chose to violently scream and hit us until we packed into the car. Most of the time, someone was rubbing a sore arm or wiping away tears as we drove to Mass. And then automatically, as if a button had been pushed, we would march respectfully into the church. I hated going to church. Although I enjoyed the value of a good sermon, I hated seeing the hypocrisy of our mother. She warmly greeted parishioners and looked for their adulation and respect in lining up seven children who were so well behaved and coiffed. Little did they know that four hours of verbal and physical abuse had taken place prior to our arriving at our destination.

I would stare at our mother, wondering how she could pull off such a farce. Her Academy Award performance was amazing, and she felt no remorse for her behavior or guilt for her actions on a holy day. As soon as Mass was over and we packed back into our car, the abuse would begin again. She shot from her mouth cutting, assaultive verbal adjectives toward us every Sunday—stupid, ugly, and lazy were her favorites. And she said the "f" word constantly. No one was exempt from the lash of her tongue or the strike of her hand.

My father generally made himself oblivious to the anger by removing himself as soon as the car stopped in the driveway. He'd run for cover, busying himself in the yard or garage. Every Sunday was a nightmare.

Since it was difficult to pray in our mother's presence, I said short prayers in my head. I begged God to stop the abuse. I begged God to kill her so that we would be free. I prayed that I would go to sleep and not wake up. I prayed to learn to take care of myself and to live far, far away. I would say the words from the Beatles' song: "Help, I need somebody / Help, not just anybody." I questioned whether or not the God we learned about in church or any god for that matter was listening.

———•———

WITH CHILDREN COMES WORK. OUR mother did an exceptional job cleaning our clothes, getting us to the dentist, and making sure we had good schooling. What she lacked was the warmth and soothing touch of a protector. She armed herself with certain "weapons" to use on us, such as wooden spoons, horse whips, shoes, batons, forks, and potato mashers. She grabbed just about anything she could get her hands on.

All of us were tiny, weighing no more than forty-five pounds in the fourth grade, so the tools used to keep us in line hurt. One of my brothers weighed twenty-two pounds in kindergarten. When we heard the cupboard where wooden spoons were held clinging, we ran for cover. We would try to warn each other to get ready for the hitting. We would mentally and physically prepare ourselves for the anger of our mother. Not a day went by that was free of her rage. We never experienced one day without being hit or beaten or bruised or verbally abused. It was exhausting.

Our mother always mentioned that one of the most frustrating things for her was the fact that none of us threw each other under the bus. If she wanted to know who deserved the beating for not sweeping the garage perfectly, none of us turned the "guilty party" in. She would end up hitting all of us, but she never got the answers she desired. Each one of us could have made excellent prisoners of war. We would never divulge anything to the detriment of someone else. This infuriated her and it gave us satisfaction to know she'd lost that battle with us.

CHAPTER NINE

———◆———

OCCUPYING THE BRAIN AND SEEING
FEAR IN HER OWN FACE

BATON TWIRLING FIT RIGHT IN with us because our mother truly believed that children should never idle. Early in our childhood, she enrolled her oldest three daughters in baton twirling classes. Our initial introductions to the sport were in the hall above the fire department. We got measured for batons and met our instructor. I was intrigued by this instrument. I watched in amazement as older girls performed with such energy and grace. Several of the girls wore medals and showed off their accolades. Then our instructor walked in. She was so pretty and bubbly. Her name was Joanne, and I thought she was the prettiest girl/woman I had ever seen. She dropped down to eye level and introduced herself to the three of us. She was wearing heavy eye makeup and had beautiful, long hair, not the stern look of our mother. She was beautiful, and I immediately began to pray that I would grow up and look just like her. Comparatively, she resembled the actress Ann Margret.

When you are young and being physically abused, when you come across a kind soul like Miss Joanne, you cling to the feelings as a coping mechanism. You dream of this person being part of your permanent life. You melt away with the enormity of the normalcy. It brightens your day and gives you something to look forward to.

Our mother signed us up for multiple lessons, performances, and parades. As youngsters, we would be part of the Tiny Tots, the youngest of twirlers. We had fun, and the activity distracted our mother. She could not lash out at us if we were on a stage or marching in a parade. We could concentrate on the art of baton twirling, instead of the art of running from our mother. We also could surround ourselves in the presence of a warm human being, very much like we did when around our grandmother.

Mitzy, Tricia, and I eagerly awaited the days of our lessons with Miss Joanne. She was sweet and smelled good like our grandmother. On one particular evening, our father entered the rehearsal area and motioned to the three of us that he was there to pick us up but would wait for us in his car. At that moment, Miss Joanne asked us if the man was our father. We said yes. She immediately ran behind a mirrored billboard, and I could see her applying lipstick and combing her long, blond hair. She asked us if he was picking us up. We said yes. Then she said something that made me dream of a new life. She said, "He is cute! I will walk you out to your father's car."

She approached my father's car, and for the first time, I witnessed flirting. She was bubbling over with energy, and Dad was smitten. After introductions, Miss Joanne opened the door, glided us into the car, and said good-bye.

While driving home, our father asked, "Holy smokes, is that your instructor?"

We replied, en masse, "Yes, that is Miss Joanne, and she said you were cute."

Our father replied, "Well, I guess I will be picking you girls up more often."

Someone had said he was cute. The adjective was so much more pleasant than the adjectives heard in our house. Cute. To this day, the word *cute* embodies much, much more than just a word. Every time I hear or speak the word, I think of that moment between my father and Miss Joanne.

After baton lessons, we took baths, and as I lay in the bathtub in the green bathroom, the bathroom where I was attacked by our mother, I dreamed of having Miss Joanne as my mother. I wanted my father and Miss Joanne to get married so we could have her forever. We needed to be free of the witch who occupied my father's bed. We needed Miss Joanne desperately.

I think that, when abuse is occurring, many children, like I did, fantasize about a more peaceful family environment. This is another coping mechanism. It is a child's way of reaching toward normalcy. In my brain, I observed many women who would have made perfect mates for my father. Since he was such a gentleman, why could he not perfect his life and gravitate toward someone who was just as sweet and elegant? Did he not deserve that? Why he did not excise our mother from his life baffled me for years. He never knew what it was like to be married to a loving person who adored him. He settled for far, far less. He got the short end of the stick with her as his wife and we got shortchanged with having this mean woman as our mother.

ON NOVEMBER 22, 1962, ONE of the women residing adjacent to our school property was watching television and listening to her radio and heard that President Kennedy had been shot. In a panic, she came into our school screaming and yelling, "President Kennedy has been shot. President Kennedy has been shot."

We were instructed to kneel down and say a few prayers.

About half an hour later, the same woman came running back into the school again yelling, "President Kennedy is dead. President Kennedy is dead."

It was the second time I felt fear—the first time true fear had crept through me since our mother had beaten me and Mitzy after we'd Ajaxed the kitchen table. I can still see this woman running down the halls with her white apron on, screaming in disbelief that our beloved president had been assassinated.

For the next several weeks, there were no baton lessons. The world seemed to stand still when President Kennedy was shot. Our mother was transfixed by the television. She would repeat, "I cannot believe this happened to Jackie Kennedy." She said it in a way that suggested she personally knew the first lady. I presume that, since the Kennedys were so vital and attractive and had small children, Americans like our mother could connect. It was unusual to see a sympathetic reaction from our mother. I would have expected a remark like, "He must have deserved it." After all, our mother had sympathy for only a few.

We did not attend school for a bit until the country settled down. Our mother did not beat us during that time. She was engrossed with the national news. If anything good transpired from the assassination, it was the fact that we were not beaten during that time.

WHEN BATON LESSONS RESUMED, I became a fanatic and became quite thin. If I practiced my moves on our patio, our mother left me alone. In fact, I think she thought I was quite good. Years went by, and I would rush home from school and just grab that baton and head to the patio to get away from her.

When I was fifteen years old, I won a special contest, whereby one girl was selected from each state to perform at Notre Dame University. My instructor, Jan, accompanied me. Unfortunately, prior to leaving for Indiana, I ate a yogurt that was spoiled and became quite ill. Jan took me to the emergency room. A physician came into the room and examined my naked body and asked me to step on the scale. I weighed ninety-four pounds. He asked me how old I was, and I replied that I was almost sixteen years old. He asked me when I'd had my last period, and I replied that I had yet to have my period. Then he looked me square in the eye and asked me how many times I threw up in one day, and I replied that I had been throwing up since I left Maryland. Bewildered, he rephrased the question and asked me if I purposefully made myself throw up.

"Why would I want to do that?" I asked.

"You are too thin for your age," he replied. "Girls do this all the time to stay thin."

"Everyone in my family is thin," I told him. "My dad is a jockey."

To this day, I do not think the doctor believed one thing coming out of my mouth. Nevertheless, it was the first time I'd heard mention of anorexia and bulimia among the general populace. I thought only jockeys threw up. I did not do anything to keep my weight down.

Upon returning home, I repeated the story about the emergency room visit.

"I can't believe you have not had your period," our mother said.

She took me to our pediatrician, who requested that she take me to Georgetown University Hospital for an examination. I remember at the time—and this was prior to the confidentiality required today—that an unprofessional woman took my intake sheet, looked at it, and yelled across the reception area, "Tracey Cooper, you said you have not had a period. Are you pregnant?"

I remember feeling completely embarrassed by that question. Our mother looked at me in horror. She was relieved that I replied no. I was still a virgin.

The examining physician told our mother that my anatomy was completely normal. Driving home, I asked our mother what the doctors thought they might have discovered, and she said, "They thought you might be missing your female parts."

How horrible! No female parts!

We returned to our regular doctor, and he looked our mother in the eye and said, "This child will get her period if you allow her to sit and do nothing for the next several months. No cleaning the house, no baton practice, nothing. I do not want her to move! Additionally, you must feed her brownies every day. When she gains weight, believe me, she will get her period." He was not talking to our mother; he was commanding our mother. For the first time, I saw her take an order outside her own opinion or control.

To my amazement, our mother obeyed the doctor's instructions, and for the next several months, I sat and sat and sat. It was glorious. No cleaning. No polishing her furniture. No scrubbing. No vacuuming. No sweeping. No practicing. I hated cleaning her house. I hated that my sweat was adding to the farce of perfection that clouded the reality of what was occurring among the furniture.

Ultimately, I got my period and life resumed.

CHAPTER TEN

TRICIA AT AGE SIXTEEN

MY OLDER SISTER TRICIA, AT an early age, found a way of coping with the abuse. Her mechanism was to become combative; she would take a stance and not let go. She repeatedly yelled back at our mother, repeatedly stood her ground, and reminded our mother that she hated her. Therefore, Tricia received the most brutal beatings. She was like a fractious race horse, unable to be tamed, which drove our mother nuts. She went toe to toe with our mother. They collided like gladiators, and the victor was, unfortunately, our mother. Tricia never laid a finger on her during the beatings, but she lashed out with her tongue and disregard. She took her beatings and accepted her bruises. On the other hand, our mother felt defeated due to Tricia's unyielding attitude and the fact that she remained vocal and expressed disdain for the abuse.

During my childhood, I always thought that one of the "gladiators" would die, but I did not quite know which gladiator. It would not have surprised me if there was a death. In fact, it seemed inevitable. Nonetheless, Tricia's defiance tortured our mother just as much as the beatings tortured Tricia. She began to stay up late, to remain at school dances longer than permitted, and to simply defy the rules.

Tricia tried to avoid moving to Delaware with the family during the Delaware racing meet. She softened her stance with our mother when she begged our mother to allow her best friend, Michelle, to come with us to Delaware. Our mother agreed on the condition that Tricia behave and not talk back.

None of us knew at the time that Tricia was sneaking around with the motel lifeguard, a cute guy named Joe, who had been accepted to the University of Delaware. Since he was a few years older than Tricia, he knew how to get around Delaware. At the Gateway Motor Inn, Tricia and I had a motel room to ourselves while our parents and the other siblings occupied the efficiency; it was our home away from home during the summer Delaware racing meet.

One evening, Tricia and Michelle arranged to meet up with Joe. But first, they had to get past our mother. They walked down to the efficiency to say good night to her and then came back to the room, arranged their bed as if they were sleeping in it, and then giggled their way out to Joe's awaiting car.

Sure enough, about an hour later, I heard a key in the door. Pretending to be in a deep sleep, I heard our mother click the light switch on. Then she kicked my bed and asked, "Where the hell did your sister and Michelle go? Tell me before I knock your head off."

I pretended like I was waking up, sat up, and said, "I have no idea. When I went to bed, they were brushing their teeth. Are they not in bed?"

I did not get my sentence out fast enough. She took that damn Daniel Green slipper of hers off and began hitting me with it.

I kept saying, "I don't know. I don't know."

She was not buying my story, so she summoned my father to continue the interrogation. He reluctantly yelled at me to tell him where they went. I continued covering for Tricia and said, "Dad, I have no idea."

My father left, and our mother continued to slap me, pull my hair, kick me, and step on my toes. She hit my back, my legs, my face, and my arms. She was so frustrated that her anger went through her brain to her fists and onto my skin. I simply would not confess, for I knew Tricia would be beaten worse than me.

Our mother decided to remain in our room, and at about 2:00 in the morning, Michelle and Tricia walked in. Our mother went into full-scale nut mode. She took Tricia by the hair and threw her around the room. Frightened, Michelle ran to the farthest corner of the room. Now and then during the encounter, Tricia would glance at me as if to say, *What did you tell her?*

Our mother kept screaming that she would not stop hitting Tricia until she told her where she had been. The slapping and the kicking and the pulling of the hair went on for quite some time. Tricia was determined not to say where she'd gone. She kept repeating, "We were just hanging out."

Our mother would scream, "Stop lying to me, you little son of a bitch."

Tricia never folded. She was covering for Joe. Our mother surely would have gotten him fired from his lifeguard job at the pool and then made his life miserable. Tricia knew that.

During the entire beating, I wondered what Michelle was thinking. Over the years, we'd mentioned the beatings to Michelle, but she'd said that she thought our mother was wonderful. Now it was irrefutable.

When our mother finally weakened and left the room, Michelle started to cry. She had witnessed the brutality. She kept apologizing to Tricia for promoting the evening with Joe. Poor Michelle had no idea how our mother would react. I knew. I knew from the moment the two of them padded their bed that a beating was in store. They should have known that they could not outfox the evil one. She was always three steps ahead of us.

Joe was so upset the next morning when Michelle filled him in on our mother's rage. He saw the bruises and the scratches on Tricia and slowly pulled away from hanging out with her. He was from a normal family. I think he ran from Tricia because he did not want to be responsible for more injury to her. Tricia liked him. Tricia was just being a normal dumb teenager who wanted to stretch out a bit. She muttered, "This is the last time that witch of a mother drives a boy away from me."

That afternoon, Tricia told Michelle and I to get in the car. She was in a weird mood. We drove around the Delaware farmland, and Tricia led the car into rows and rows of crops. For some reason, she had a moment of insanity. She decided to kick up the radio and drive as fast as she could while creating circles in this poor farmer's crops. She kept going around and around and around. Michelle and I kept telling her to stop, but she was out of control. I started to think she was imagining the crops as our mother's head, and she was bound and determined to crush her. She had to get it out. She was a mess. She was damaged goods and needed to just scream it out.

The owner of the land saw Tricia, took down her license number, and reported the incident to the police. A local policeman recognized the family name and knew jockeys routinely stayed at the Gateway Motor Inn during track season. We got a knock on the door, and a policeman informed our mother of the incident.

Instead of beating Tricia again, our mother put her and Michelle in the car and drove Michelle back to Maryland. Our mother was probably too weak to beat her within an inch of her life again so soon; it was easier to just drive a hundred miles an hour and throw Michelle onto her family driveway.

Chapter Eleven

---◆---

The Handprint

We had several cousins who were prone to getting into trouble. One was Matthew. At age thirteen, he decided to break into a theatre and a gas station. My grandmother told our mother that she needed Matthew to come to Maryland for the summer in an attempt to straighten himself out.

Our mother was enraged because she did not want to take on another child. She cursed my grandmother, and she cursed thirteen-year-old Matthew. Yet we prepared for Matthew's arrival. We presumed he was a tyrant; a criminal; a bad, bad child. We would never break into a gas station or theatre. Who did that? Only bad people, really bad people did such things. Each of us vowed to lock our bedroom doors at night to protect ourselves from such a human being.

Upon Matthew's arrival, we were enthralled with him—this nervy bad boy. Once the new arrival had settled in the bedroom he would share with Buddy, we asked him why he'd broken into the gas station and theatre. His reply? "I just wanted candy." Just wanted candy? Poor thing. His father had abandoned him. His mother had abandoned him, and now he simply wanted candy. He did not seem violent. He did not seem fierce. He appeared to be a normal kid, albeit one without boundaries or guidance. But his parents blessed him with movie star good looks, and we could not stop staring at how beautiful he was.

As Matthew made himself comfortable in our home, our mother's anxiety and stress began to elevate. We sat Matthew down and warned him about her wrath. We told him to be good, use manners, keep his room tidy, not touch the walls, and help with things like sweeping the garage. Of utmost importance was to obey her.

Matthew was not immune from our mother's anger. One day, he did not obey the ringing of the bell for all of us to cease what we were doing and to run home. It was an innocent error on his part. Once he'd made it home, late for dinner, our mother demanded that he go to his room as punishment.

After dinner, I heard our mother's footsteps going up the stairs toward Matthew. I quietly followed and peered into the room, and I witnessed my mother slap Matthew across the face. Matthew began to cry. As if this poor child needed more sadness in his life. He had been dissected from his family, and now our mother was terrorizing him. He was only thirteen years old. He only wanted candy. Our mother could not drum up any compassion for this child. Instead of repairing his little broken spirit, instead of guiding him into becoming a productive person, our mother lashed out at him. She stormed out of the bedroom, feet slamming down on every step to the first floor.

I tiptoed into Matthew's room and saw tears rolling down his eyes and a deep handprint on his delicate, white skin. He felt humiliated. I sat down with him and asked him what had provoked the evil one.

Choking back his tears, he said, "I did not hear the bell ... And then, when I got home, Auntie found my tackle box and fishing pole. I did not know we were not allowed to go to the reservoir."

The reservoir! On no! Memories of Buddy getting hit by the car flooded my mind. Matthew threw himself on the bed and cried for his mother. His tears rolled down his face. I wondered why on earth his mother, Linda, had left him. Why would she leave her three boys? It seemed so out of line for her to do such a thing. If she could see her son with a palm print on his face and tears streaming down his face, would she come home and caress him?

Our mother could only stand a few weeks with Matthew. She resented having to care for him, so we packed up the station wagon and took him back to New Hampshire.

Years later, Matthew and his brother, Luke, sadly became addicted to heroin. As they shared their needles, they unfortunately were among the first casualties of the AIDS epidemic. As Matthew lay dying on his bed, his last words were cries out for his mother.

AS WE GREW UP AND our mother aged, she naturally got weaker. While we were now too large to get hit, she became too weak to continue her physical assaults anyway. Her tongue and her punishments were her only weapons left to her accord. So when the youngest became a teenager, the physical trauma she received was less than what we older children had been dealt.

But Baby Sister was not immune from our mother's anger, and she too felt the law of punishment dealt by our mother. One day, for some reason, Baby decided to drink wine at a friend's wedding. When she came home, she threw up about a million times. When our mother asked her what she had consumed, she honestly told our mother that she'd drank some wine. Our mother gave her the harshest punishment on our family record. There was no beating, no horse whip, no potato masher, and no wooden spoon to be thrust upon her small body. Baby's punishment was to remain in her bedroom for one year. So, when Baby came home from school, she walked right upstairs to her bedroom only to come out for meals or a bath or to attend school.

Since Baby had no socialization or television for a year, she decided to read every book in the room. She read and read and read, and when Baby came out at the end of her sentence, she was able to graduate from high school at age fifteen. When she ranked number one in her master of laws program and graduated from law school summa cum laude, she attributed her excellent study skills to the punishment. Her reading paid off, and she became a great student and a great lawyer.

CHILDREN WHO VISITED OUR HOME also had to "fly right" if they were to be asked back. They dried dishes, were forced to exhibit manners, and sometimes got the brunt force of the wooden spoon. Undeterred, the visitors weighed their options. They enjoyed our company so much that if they too got hit by our mother, it did not matter. They knew they could go home if it got too heated—unlike us; we were trapped.

All of us were attractive and energetic and fun. Where we got our compassion and graciousness is hard to imagine since we were physically abused almost daily. I truly feel that each one of us got the tenacity and grace of our father. We got our energy from our mother but thankfully not much more. We were not reclusive. We became ambitious competitors. We were cohesive even during the beatings. As teenagers, we kept our "no snitching" rule. Our mother would constantly remark that we protected each other and how impossible it was for her to figure out which child spilled the milk or put a smear on the walls. We never snitched on one another, which ticked her off. And we enjoyed being able to inflict on her frustration.

As we came into our own personas, it was nice to see her weaken. Her hands were becoming gnarled with arthritis. Her walk was slower even though her health was good. She began to sit more and not fixate on us as much. She started reaching out to us as adults, which was confusing. She listened to the new things we learned and the events of the day. Due to her abuse, we were not receptive to any type of warmth from her. We simply felt nothing. Oddly, we felt a weird respect for her. Maybe the commandment that had been impregnated in our minds was to blame. "Honor thy mother."

CHAPTER TWELVE

A BROKEN HEART AND A WILL TO HEAL

As WE GREW UP, OUR mother's pattern was the same. We just became used to it. We knew what she was like. We knew what set her off. We knew how void of warmth she was. We also learned what attrition of the soul felt like. Nonetheless, we grew up. Although carrying out physical attacks against us became more difficult for her as we grew in size, her verbal abuse continued. The older children were not physically assaulted once they stood eye to eye with her. The assaults against the smaller children continued.

In 1972, I was fifteen years old and experienced one of my last beatings. It ensued from an argument I had with Mitzy over a china bowl. Upon waking for school, I descended the stairs to quickly eat a bowl of cereal. Mitzy was sitting in front of the cabinets obstructing access. She repeatedly stated that she was not moving, so I pushed her aside. She dramatically moaned, which brought our mother to the forefront. Our mother, her eyes bulging out of her head, grabbed a potato masher and began to beat me with it. As her strikes came down upon my body, I reflected that this beating was just as bad as the one I'd received years ago in the green bathroom. I remember thinking that I could no longer take it. I wanted to be done with her presence, done with being her target, done with her anger. I was so sick of the attacks in a venue that was supposed to be an oasis of familial gatherings and loving embraces. I felt like I was fading away, that life was too cruel a system. I wanted out, or I wanted to simply die in my sleep.

As usual, with bruises and bad memories, I gathered the strength to get to school and put on my happy face. I wondered if I could keep up the facade and was bewildered at how often the teachers and nuns complimented our mother. It was nauseating to hear them say, "Your mother is the most energetic person I have ever met," or, "Your mother is wonderful." Her public persona was nothing like the teeth-clenching terror she conveyed. She was always so angry that her eyes seemed to bulge from her head and realign her face.

AFTER SCHOOL, WHILE AVOIDING OUR mother as best I could, I forced myself to fill my brain with better thoughts than the next beating. I loved admiring my trophies and folding my beauty pageant banners into my box under my bed. I put congratulatory notes, newspaper articles, perfect report cards, and diaries in my memento box. Looking at the items was a reminder of something positive and healthy. It gave me great joy to float away while looking at them.

On last count, I had acquired over 350 baton trophies. I'd worked hard to achieve each one. As the trophies had begun to occupy too much space in my bedroom, I had to move them to our basement. My father constructed shelving in the basement, and I carried the trophies down and gingerly placed them atop the shelves. I was proud that I'd won so many awards. Every one of them brought a smile to my face.

The trophies were neatly assembled. I dusted them off weekly because our mother hated dust. In addition to the trophies for baton twirling, I had won academic awards at the end of each school year. We all had. Additionally, in my senior year, I had my eyes set on entering the Junior Miss contest to obtain scholarship money for college. If I won the title, I perhaps could afford to go away to college. To be eligible for the Junior Miss contest, I had to have a great cumulative GPA, which I had. I also recognized that I would be judged on a talent and an interview with a panel of judges. I thought I could ace both.

To help me win the Junior Miss contest, I dug in and got involved in the student government, became president of the National Honor Society, kept my grades up, and tried out for the cheerleading squad. I was popular with the geeks and, ultimately, with the jocks. Dating was limited; I couldn't allow myself to be sidetracked. My mother was strict. Only certain people were allowed in our home.

TRICIA WAS A CHEERLEADER AND developed a few platonic boyfriends. One of them, Paul Wayne, came to our house one day. I was not as forward as Tricia and distanced myself from "boy encounters." When Paul walked in the door, I thought he was the cutest boy I had ever seen, and he had a little twinkle in his eye. He enjoyed Tricia's company, and I was jealous. I could hear them laughing and joking while watching television in the family room. Often, Paul would arrive with a classmate named Dale. Dale lived in the same neighborhood as Paul. Both boys were very nice, and they made a fun duo of change in our home.

Months went by. My crush continued, but Paul did not notice me until I got my braces off and became a cheerleader, a maneuver to get him to notice me and a way to attend the games with the basketball team, which he was a part of. It was such a glorious time. It was fun.

On our first away game on the bus, Paul saw me and asked, "What are you doing on the bus?"

"I am on the cheerleading squad," I told him.

He took a seat behind me just to stare. I listened to his laughter and his jokes with his friend and teammate John. John was dating another cheerleader. *How convenient*, I thought. Somehow, from that moment on, I knew Paul would one day be my boyfriend.

Paul and I started dating when he asked if he could drive me home one day.

"Tricia is not home," I replied.

"That is not why I am driving you home," he said. Then he grabbed my hand and held it until he got to my driveway. I had never held a boy's hand, and it was so nice that I did not let go. Paul could have had any girl in our school because he was extremely popular. I was so happy he was holding *my* hand.

Paul became a reprieve from our mother's anger.

The longer Paul and I dated, the more he could see what was going on in the house. He always saw the bruises, and he saw the pain. He would look so helpless when he dropped me off at the door. He could do nothing about what he knew awaited me inside except kiss me and make me laugh it all away. He treated me well. I adored him. I fantasized about marrying him and having a home with him and just shutting the door and never letting our mother in. He made a habit of driving me home, and I would insist that he drive slowly. The slower he drove, the more time I had with him. We were both very cognizant that the dragon was home, and neither of us wanted to see the fire from her nostrils, so we always went straight home.

Paul's father was a huge man with a Japanese heritage. His mom looked Irish. She was tiny. I never saw them together without Paul's father embracing his mother. He always held her close. They laughed all the time and were constantly touching each other. It was wonderful to witness.

One evening, after a basketball game, Paul drove me to his home. All of the lights were out, and when we opened the front door, his parents were slowly dancing to the music of the Platters. I just stared. I wanted the same life. I wanted the house, the Platters, and the love of holding Paul's hand. I wanted to get out of my home so desperately. I wanted normal. I wanted to just lay in bed and kiss Paul the rest of my life, have a few babies, and think pleasant thoughts. He pressed the issue of sex and eventually that happened but we were scared to death that the "tormentor" would find out. I could not even imagine the price to be paid for merely loving someone.

MY HOPES AND DREAMS WERE dashed when Paul sat me down in the yard of our school one cold day in December and told me that he had gotten another girl in high school pregnant. I wanted to just lay down and die as he spoke to me. My heart was breaking with every word. He looked me directly in the eye. He told me he had been drunk when he'd had sex with her. He'd driven the girl home and had stayed until it was dark. He said the girl had turned the lights out and the sex had just happened. She was planning on having an abortion, and Paul had told her father that he'd gotten his daughter pregnant. He said he needed to console her. He still cared for me. I heard the words *drunk, dark, sex, pregnant, abortion.* These words were too much to handle from the mouth of the boy I adored. I just sat there listening intently. I was like a flower dying in the heat. I wilted and died.

At the end of this devastating conversation, I promised Paul that I would not tell anyone, especially since we were Catholic. At that moment, I wished I had a warm mother to run to. The woman who bore me was such a blistering person that she would surely beat me if I'd attempted any discussion of what had happened. I could barely concentrate for the rest of the day. As classes changed, I saw the pregnant girl in the hall, and she saw me. She knew Paul had told me.

She looked at me somewhat apologetically. She was probably in love with him. I looked at her sympathetically. Although I had nothing in common with her, now we had a mutual bond—Paul.

I drove by Kitty's home and did not see her car in the driveway. I wanted so desperately to talk to someone who would not scold me or strike me. Since Kitty was not available, I scrambled back home and went for the only safe place of solace I could find, my memento box. I pulled my memento box from under my bed and wanted to just read the cards and letters that Bob had written me. This box represented happiness. The contents consisted of pressed prom flowers, cards and notes, and trinkets that represented normal. While going through the contents of that box, I could dream and imagine a pretty life, a happy existence. I wanted Paul's love back. I wanted the words that he'd said to me to go away.

When I opened the box I was aghast. Our mother stepped into my room and announced, "That box was too full, so I threw all those things away." Threw my things away?

She had thrown things away that gave me great joy. At that moment, I looked up and saw the look in her eye; I ran down to the basement to see if my trophies were secure. I could not believe my eyes. She followed me down the stairs and said, "I was tired of those fucking trophies, so I gave them to a charity."

"Even my first trophy?" I asked. "Even my state trophy?"

I hated her more than I ever had. I simply thought she was the worst human being on earth. I recalled the neighbor child sitting on the school bus watching Baby get beaten—the one who had called her "the meanest mother in the neighborhood." His proclamation was so on point. Not only did I lose my boyfriend, I also lost all my precious mementos. My relationship with Paul was torn to shreds, and my heart was broken. I seriously considered ending my life.

I think I must have been a relatively strong person to keep going. After I cried my eyes out in silence, I ate my dinner with my family and excused myself to do homework. Instead of homework, I just sat at my desk and continued to cry. I talked to myself and prayed. I prayed for Paul and I prayed for the girl who was carrying his child. I thought about my lovely father and how disappointed he would be if I took my life. I thought about how I was to graduate from high school in a year and how maybe, just maybe, I could get accepted to a college far from home. I knew our mother would prefer me to stay at home while I attended college. That way, she could continue to target me. But I told myself that I would be able to convince her to allow me to attend a school away from home as long as it wasn't too far away.

I lay on my bed, feeling crushed by everything that happened. Then suddenly, I rose up and said, "She should die, not me. She should get cancer and die."

I vowed to stay alive so I could spit on her grave. I fantasized about seeing her, not me, in the coffin. My thoughts began to shift. Instead of praying for my soul, I prayed that she would die. I began to believe in myself and the desire to rise above her. Then, as an act of defiance, I walked into our mother's bedroom and hid her wedding ring. I just took it from her jewelry box, and I walked it to a hiding place, I said, "This piece of jewelry will never touch my body again."

After recovering from Paul's destructive actions, I knew clearly that I was fading as a human being. I simply could not take any more of our mother's abuse on top of a broken heart. I vowed to make an appointment with my guidance counselor and plan my college days. I also disavowed our mother. I walked down the stairs, looked at our mother while she was ironing in the kitchen, and said, "Kitty Carson would never have thrown my trophies and mementos away. I feel like she is more of a mother than you. Nothing I do makes you happy. Nothing I do makes you cheer for me. I am exhausted. I am tired of cleaning your home. The nuns adore me. My teachers adore me. You simply hate me. I don't know why, but you do. Mothers should not hate their good daughters."

Our mother stared at me. I stood straight and looked her directly in the eye. I hated her.

That evening, I cried my eyes to sleep. I tossed and turned and wondered if I would die of bad memories. I felt helpless. I felt controlled by our mother, but I knew that if I got out, I would no longer have to deal with her actions and her abuse. I needed to get out. I could not stay and worry about my siblings because I felt like I was dying. I knew I was a good person. I knew I was smart. I knew I was becoming more attractive. I had to get out. I was determined to run straight out the door as soon as I was equipped to do so. I needed to live, not die.

CHAPTER THIRTEEN

———◆———

ENTER BROTHER-IN-LAW

IN 1974, AS OUR MOTHER'S physical assaults were lessening because we had grown too big to beat, a wonderful blessing occurred. My father brought five-time Kentucky Derby winner, Bill Hartack to dinner, and for some reason, Bill stayed in our home for several months. Our mother put on a better face for Bill than I had ever witnessed in front of other public individuals. She seemed happy. She pranced around and felt like it was an honor to have such a famous person staying with us. Due to Bill's status, our mother laughed and never screamed in his presence. His presence was a blessing, and it was a reprieve from the beatings and anger.

One day after a long day of racing, Bill reached out to Tricia and asked her if she would be interested in going on a date with a new rider. She was in her senior year of high school. Interested, she said yes. Bill mentioned that the "kid" had talent, that he was from the Midwest, and he was good-looking.

So on a quiet day, the doorbell rang, and in walked my future brother-in-law, who I will call "Talent." Bill was correct in his assessment. Talent had big, brown eyes and a lot of brown hair and was very handsome. He had an obvious scar on his cheek that was in the shape of a horseshoe. Talent was brave enough to come to our house. I presumed he'd heard the stories that Dad was easygoing and our mother was a bit tough. Many race trackers who came to our home witnessed our mother's "strong" way of handling things, and I was sure Talent had been forewarned by one of them before entering our home.

Naturally, Tricia took an instant liking to Talent, and for the next several months, the two were inseparable. This was 1974, and she was only seventeen years old and still in high school, but things between them moved quickly. She would travel with him to various racetracks, and he won quite a few races. The only time my father stepped in and forbid her movement was in relation to a man named Dan, who owned many horses that Talent rode. Dan had a bad reputation around the racetrack. He was involved with drugs and prostitutes, and my father laid down the law—Tricia was not to go anywhere with him.

Talent's career began to soar; he was becoming an outstanding rider, and he was consistently put on good horses. Unfortunately, the more Tricia's relationship with Talent intensified, the more volatile her relationship with our mother became. Our mother craved control like people crave chocolate candy bars. Control was her oxygen. She needed it. Without control, our mother went out of control. She needed to control her children, to keep the "fence" around them so that she knew every step they took and their exact whereabouts. Tricia proved to be on her own schedule, not our mother's timeline for her. Tricia was just as unbridled as some of the fractious race horses, and she paid a price for the character trait.

Like me, Tricia had thoughts of leaving home, but her path to do so opened up ahead of mine. She'd had enough. One day, she looked our mother in the eye and said, "When I turn eighteen, I am leaving."

"You are going nowhere," our mother screamed. "You are going to college."

"I hate you, and I am not living here anymore," Tricia refused to back down and screamed, "I will be marrying Talent."

And thus, a war began. For the next ten months, every night on cue, Tricia and our mother screamed at one another. Doors slammed. Skin got slapped. The yelling was continuous. Tricia bore the bruises of the conflicts. She did not care how hard she got hit or how loud our mother got. She knew that she would soon be on her own, and she just let the time go by before she was finally out the door. I was amazed at her resolve. She hated our mother and always screamed, "I will be gone soon, and you will no longer be able to hit or control me."

TRICIA MARRIED TALENT TEN DAYS after she turned eighteen. She was free. She was done. She was legal. She did not have to deal with our mother. She was a bird that could fly away. I was so envious. I remember crying myself to sleep the night of her wedding, wondering if I was normal, wondering if Tricia would be normal after all the child abuse.

Knowing she could not change Tricia's mind, our mother prepared a small wedding service at St. Mary's Catholic Church and a reception at our home. Not many people attended due to the friction between Tricia and our mother. Nonetheless, Talent's mother came in from out of state, and I was the maid of honor, with one of Talent's friends standing as his best man.

After the religious ceremony, the get-together at our home was very sweet, and Tricia and Talent left to spend the night at a local hotel prior to going on their honeymoon.

Tricia looked great. She was thin and blond and looked more like a woman than a young schoolgirl. She also looked thrilled. She would be a nice addition to Talent as his career took off. It didn't hurt that she'd come from Bud's brood of children. This would endear race trackers to Talent even more and give him an additional seal of approval within the racing industry.

The following morning, Talent and Tricia stopped by the house to gather up a few things. The house still evidenced signs that something happy had taken place. There were bits of white decorations here and there and photographs and flowers throughout the home. It all seemed a bit blissful. Then all of a sudden, our mother went into a rampage, verbally attacking them. Apparently, they had left the wedding reception without saying good-bye to her. For that, they got a piece of her mind. The home, once again, was a place of yelling and conflict.

I peered into the kitchen where our mother was berating the newlyweds, and I glanced at Talent. He looked so striking and put together while standing there accepting the verbal assaults being shot at him. He was holding Tricia's hand. I knew he would protect her, but I also knew at that moment that they were doomed. Without our mother's support, it would be only a matter of time. I felt sad that he was now part of this upheaval, part of our family dynamics with our mother. Upon leaving, I heard Talent lean over to Tricia and say, "We are going to get as far away from her as we possibly can."

When Tricia left, it felt like there was a death in the family, and the house got very quiet. There were no more shouting matches between Tricia and our mother. Our mother treated Tricia's early marriage as an obvious failure of her mothering. She did not want people to wonder why Tricia was flying the nest so soon. She was infuriated at Tricia and reminded Tricia of her "errors"—one being the marriage— at every opportunity she had.

During 1975, Talent rode some really great race horses. One special horse was going to be entered in a major stakes race at Pimlico. We also heard that the horse did not have a chance to win. Besides, Foolish Pleasure had just won the Kentucky Derby and had an outstanding record under the tutelage of trainer Leroy Jolley, and Talent's horse was up against a known winner. My father knew that this stakes racing card was filling up. Talent would be competing not only against some good horses but also against the best riders—Willie Shoemaker, Ron Turcotte, Lafitt Pincay, Jacinto Vasquez, and Braulio Baeza. Talent's work was cut out for him.

Nonetheless, Talent and the horse's trainer W. E. "Smiley" Adams were thrilled to be on the racing card along with nine other horses in the field. Talent's horse was considered a non-contender, or in other words, a long shot.

At the time, I was working at Pimlico Race Track on the weekends for the Harry M. Stevens Corporation on one of the food stands, namely a hot dog stand. All of my siblings worked at the track when it fit into our school and baton twirling schedule. We could make some decent money on the stands. We would end up with quite a lot of tip money from the day.

We also had to beware of the slippery individuals who would try to befriend us and do things like ask if we wanted to place a bet. Fooled, the hot dog stand girls would give these con artists some money to bet. As soon as the "runner" got the money, they would never return. They often used the same ploy to get us to hand over our money for a racing program, only for us to be to be tricked gain. The racetrack was filled with petty thieves.

Out of all the stories I heard of people being cheated on the track, none top the story that jockey Angel Cordero, Jr., told me about the time when he first arrived in the United States to ride. While Angel was admiring the Empire State Building, a man approached him, posing as a property sales agent and stating that the Empire State Building had apartments for sale. If Angel paid him money once a month for one year, at the end of the year, he would receive the deed to the apartment. Religiously, Angel met the gentleman and, upon concluding the payments, waited for the deed of conveyance. Poor

Angel had been duped, and his motto from then on was to be cautious because bad people could take advantage of you and swindle you out of money.

On this special day, I was proud that my brother-in-law was riding in such a prestigious race. But I was also very jealous. I was slaving away at the hot dog stand, while Talent and Tricia were being glorified. In fact, I had learned to tire of the hot dog stand. But I needed the money for college.

I got a real dose of how the regular female racetrack employees made money via the hotdog stand. For that day, our stand workers consisted of myself and two other female workers. We prepared ourselves for a busy, hectic day. We were there early in the morning to receive our instructions and to start greeting hungry patrons. The two women on the stand both had notably heavy Baltimore accents, no education, and children at their young ages. They were not much older than me but looked visibly hardened. I recognized them from other stands at the track.

Prior to opening the stand for service, the women approached me and said, "Want to make some real money today?"

I looked at both, cigarettes dangling from their mouths, tobacco stain on their teeth, and said, "How?"

One of them pulled the greasy trash can close to the stand and said, "Well, the soda cups are counted, and at the end of the day, the number of cups sold are added together with the number of pizza slices and the number of hot dog rolls and hot dogs to compute our sales and ensure we are not stealing."

I told her that I was aware of the computations and that I did not steal.

At times, when the stands were short on money at the end of the day, all the employees on that particular stand had their paychecks deducted. The deduction had happened to me on a few occasions, and I resented it. For the thief, it was a win. If he or she stole sixty dollars, the loss would be divided by three. The thief would still be up forty dollars, having only been deducted twenty dollars.

"When a customer throws their soda cup in that trash can, if they don't smash the cup, we will take it out and reuse it but pocket the money because that cup has already been counted," the girl continued.

I stared at her and immediately replied that I could not possibly partake in that.

She looked at me and said, "So I guess you're not in?"

"No," I told her. Then I excused myself to go to the bathroom.

When I came out of my stall, both women were leaning against the sink, cigarettes in hand. "Tracey, you are not going to cause any trouble for us, are you?" one asked.

"No, I am not going to cause any trouble for you, but it is not sanitary for you to do what you plan on doing."

"Ok, we will wash out the cups," replied the other girl.

I had never heard of anything so gross, but I was too young and scared to report them.

The day was crazy. We sold a ton of hot dogs, and the two girls pocketed lots of money using second-hand cups. I couldn't even look at the customers who received the recycled cups. I vowed to never return to the hot dog stands again.

As I heard the "riders up" announcement being blared over the loudspeaker, I could not find a spot to watch Talent's race. So I diligently continued my work the stand, paying more attention to the girls' tricks than to the post parade.

Once the gates opened and the horses were off, many patrons jumped onto our counter to view the race. They roared as the horses approached the finish line.

When it was over, I heard a loud cry of amazement. I asked, "Who won? Who won?"

"Talent's horse won!" a number of people among the crowd roared. "Talent's horse won!"

Talent? My God, Talent won one of America's most prestigious races. How wonderful! He won by a length, with the famous horse, Foolish Pleasure, coming in second place.

I tried desperately to view my sister during the trophy presentation, but too many people were in the way. I thought about my dad and how hard he'd worked all his life to win a race like this. However, I knew he was sitting in the jock's room as a proud father-in-law. I thought about our mother and how maybe, just maybe, this event would bring her closer to Tricia and Talent and achieve some peace, normalcy, respect, and kindness. It did not.

TRICIA AND TALENT CAME BACK to our house after the win, and our phone was ringing off the hook. They both looked so happy and so beautiful. They made an attractive couple and a formidable unit. Our mother was behaving. She too felt the enormity of what had just happened.

Then Talent looked at our mother and said, "A California-based trainer would like me to come work for him. His name is Bobby Frankel."

And with that, Tricia and Talent moved to California. Our mother did not even have time to think about it.

Talent was hugely successful. He went on to compete in many nationally known races. He was the regular rider for popular entertainment figures who owned race horses. One day, while riding at Hollywood Park, Talent rode six winners, and he repeated the feat on another day. He was repeatedly one of the nation's top money-earning jockeys.

CHAPTER FOURTEEN

EXTINGUISHING THOUGHTS OF SUICIDE

CHILDREN WHO ARE ABUSED BY their parents, in my opinion, can suffer more than children who are bullied. With a bullied child, the child can escape into their home, turn off a text or e-mail, or reach out to a parent to move him or her from the school district or situation creating the angst. Bullied children, for the most part, are victimized by people who aren't relatives. For children who are abused by a parent, there is no escape. The trauma is a constant flow, with no umbrella to reach for. The would-be protectors are the abusers. So how does a child get through that? The conflict is immense. You battle with conflicting hatred of the parent/abuser and longing for the nurturing aspect of a parent.

An adult friend told me about a young boy who was so severely abused by his mother that he was placed in foster care. The child had endured cigarette burns on his skin and burns on his scrotum and penis from being placed in a hot tub. His hands were forced to remain on oven burners which were turned on. The child was finally taken from his home and placed in foster care. When the foster mother gently placed the child into bed, he looked up at her and said, "I really miss my mommy."

The poor abused child missed the exact person who had traumatized and tortured him. This conflict is the hardest aspect of child abuse by a parent. How do you cope with the fact that part of you loves the parent or at least longs to love the parent who is harming you? Society places such a huge emphasis on maintaining familial bonds that it is difficult to reconcile the thoughts in one's brain. My own conflict has always existed. To rectify or at least lighten the conflict, I think there were many points during which therapy would have helped to ease the situation, yet I did not seek out a therapist until very late in life.

Many times during my childhood I contemplated suicide. I was so unhappy and so tired of waking up to violence. Hope was the only thing that kept me going, and I was always pleased when the bad thoughts left my brain.

An event took place which erased my thoughts of ending my own life forever. One of my father's friends, another jockey, got into trouble for deliberately "holding" his horse during a race at Bowie Race Track in 1975. My father's friend, Eric Walsh, was riding for one of the nation's leading horse trainers and was hugely successful. But unfortunately, Eric one day conspired to fix a race with several other jockeys and was indicted and convicted. He was a frequent visitor to our home, and observing Eric's depression and lack of zeal for life was eye-opening.

Our mother was very concerned for Eric. It was confusing to witness her concern for others juxtaposed with the lack of concern she displayed for her own children. She wanted to beat Buddy for riding his bicycle to the reservoir and beat me for walking in the woods when Buddy fell down the well hole. She was not in tune with our feelings when we were small children. But she put herself out there for others. She made food, ordered flowers, and rubbed their faces and hands when they needed a gentle touch. She was magnificent at being compassionate toward outsiders and not her immediate family. Those who were on the receiving end of her compassion soaked it up like a sponge and gave her nice labels like "wonderful," "sweet," and "amazing."

Nonetheless, her concerns for Eric had merit. The men, including Eric, were found guilty and sentenced to prison. While awaiting an appeal, Eric sank into severe depression.

Our mother and father routinely spoke to Eric to raise his spirits and insisted that he come to our home and eat dinner. The pressure of the indictment and adjudication weighed heavily on him. Since horse racing had made the men well-known stars, the press took a liking to reporting the crime on a daily basis. The press had something to run with, and they kept the coverage going.

Eric took out a gun one day and shot himself in the chest. The bullet ricocheted and hit his shoulder. It was the second time he'd tried to end his life. Our mother instructed each one of her children to stay with Eric and to be a presence in his home. Surely he would not attempt suicide with one of us in his home. When it was my turn to sit with Eric, he greeted me at his door with his arm in a sling. He looked awful but was pleasant and graciously let me in. He turned on the television and said that he just wanted to lie down. We chatted for a bit about my school. He mentioned that he never finished high school. I said, "That's okay, Eric. A lot of people never finished high school. Dad didn't finish high school." He smiled and then went to his bedroom.

As I sat watching his television, my eyes traveled around the room. He had many beautiful racing trophies, winners' circle pictures, and various racing artifacts on his shelves. After several hours, it seemed unlikely that Eric was going to come out of his bedroom, so I reached into my purse and wrote a note informing him that I was going home but would visit him later in the week.

A few days after my time with Eric, our mother summoned her

children to the kitchen and informed us that Eric had, in fact, killed himself. It startled me, and I never thought of ending my life again. I began to think that, no matter how bad the abuse in our household was, I would look forward to a brighter day.

I was also getting closer to legal age. The thought of turning eighteen gave me a little spring in my step.

CHAPTER FIFTEEN

---•---

BUILDING THE EXIT RAMP

I ENDED MY SENIOR YEAR of high school in 1975 with my last and final beating. I was sleeping soundly when, all of a sudden, our mother began beating me while I was still in bed. She was screaming, "Get up. Today is awards day at your school. You better be getting awards."

She hit me and hit me and hit me. I did not realize it was awards day at the high school. Our mother was never satisfied. What a pathetic human being. I was Junior Miss. I was on student government. I was a cheerleader. I was president of the National Honor Society. I even had a job and asked neither of my parents for money.

I did not push her away. I just let her strike at me and act like an idiot. I thought about how foolish she looked and how desperate she looked. Once she left my bedroom, I thought how proud I would be if my own daughter had so many accolades. I would love her. I would cherish her. I would embrace her. I would kiss her. I hoped that I had a daughter one day in order to give her the kisses I so much deserved.

I got dressed and looked at my day planner and checked off

another day before college began. I was like a prisoner checking off the days until my release. It gave me hope. I also wondered while I dressed if I would put an end to any kind of relationship with the beast. Tricia had. She stopped calling the house and she never visited or wrote.

The drive to the high school was in silence. Our mother was angry yet composed. She knew that she would be greeted by members of the community, and she knew she had to put on her happy face. She was always good at the masquerade. While parking the car, she gave me that fierce face look. Never let them see you cry. Never let them see you upset. Never get bad grades. She looked at me threateningly, as if to say, "If you get no awards and disgrace me, look for another beating."

We were allowed to put our graduation gowns on for the awards ceremony, and as I placed the gown over my head, I felt pain from my shoulders. I felt scratches and bruises beginning to appear. Like our mother, I put on my happy face and felt real joy in the comfort of my classmates.

At the awards ceremony, I won more awards than any other graduating student. As I stood up to receive my awards numerous times when I heard my name announced, I reflected on how I had developed into a people pleaser. I had to please everyone for fear of punishment. I was receiving the awards because I could not fail; I had to please. Pleasing people enabled me to achieve. I might not have been able to control our mother, but I surely could control my grades, my achievements. As I sat in my seat wondering if my left arm was broken, I turned to look at our mother, who was sitting in the parent section. She glanced at me in approval. I glanced at her and wished she would get hit by a bolt of lightning. I hated her.

When I arrived home, she demanded that I dust the family room. I remember looking at the furniture and hating it, hating the smell of Lemon Pledge she insisted I use on the furniture, and God help me if I left a streak. I hated the entire home because every inch of it was a reminder of the abuse. I hated the azalea bushes. I hated the patios. I hated the shed. I hated the yard. I hated the driveway, and I hated all her knickknacks. I was sick of this house of horrors, and I needed to plan an escape before losing my mental health.

With dust rag in hand, I began to think about marrying someone and how the two of us would be protected against her. I had been so in love with Paul and longed to have the same loving relationship we had once enjoyed. I loved the affection. I loved the caring. I loved parking on Supplee Lane, where Buddy had been hit by the car and kissing Paul and glaring at the stars. I loved how I'd never wanted to go home.

I often reflect on the awards day. I still despise her for the event, her display of anger and fury toward me beforehand. I shake my head and think about how pathetic she was and what a bad, bad mother she was. I was just a young person trapped by biological ties to a mentally unstable human being. I wish someone would have diagnosed her so that she could have received the medical help she so clearly needed. I wish someone would have confronted her. I also wish my father would have packed us all up in a car and driven away.

Since none of those events occurred, I simply used the memory of the awards day to improve my skills at being the best mother and companion that I could become. I knew on that day that I would never verbally abuse or beat my children. And to my credit, neither physical nor verbal abuse occurred in my own family home.

AFTER HIGH SCHOOL GRADUATION, FINALLY, it was my turn to go to college. It was September 1975. I was only seventeen years old, but I was ready for the academic challenge. I selected a small school called Allegany Community College in the foothills of the Allegany Mountains in Cumberland, Maryland. At one time Cumberland was Maryland's second largest city, second only to Baltimore. It was a gateway to Allegany County. It was a bustling metropolis until many of the businesses moved closer to the East

Coast. When I lived there, it was, sadly, in a depressed state. But I did not care. Today, Cumberland is one of the poorest cities in the United States. Poor or not poor, Cumberland, Maryland, would be my new experience and an oasis for me.

I dreamed of becoming a dentist, and I learned that, studying dental assisting and dental hygiene prior to dental school would make the path easier. Thus, I enrolled in a one-year dental assisting program to determine whether I would enjoy dentistry. Then I would attend the two-year dental hygiene program and on to dental school.

During the Delaware Park summer meet, a young jockey named Sammy Boulmetis, Jr., along with our mother and me, drove to Cumberland to check on housing for the dental assisting program. We knew it would be cold in the winters due to the mountains, so I was prepared for a more brutal winter than I'd been used to. Sammy kept calling Cumberland "frostbite city," and several times during the long but picturesque drive, our mother told Sammy to shut up and not discourage me.

The campus was perfect, and the town was very quaint, with its railroad tracks and many church steeples on the horizon. It had become a depressed town since the Kelly Tire Company had moved out, and the economics of the town never bounced back. Yet it still had the flavor of a bustling section of Maryland years prior. My father rode race horses in Cumberland when he was a young man. There was a racetrack called Cumberland Race Track, and many horsemen had enjoyed racing there. The riders always said it was easier to decipher a turn in one's living room than to maneuver the turns at Cumberland.

Before the classes began, I needed a dwelling to rent. There was no on-campus housing. Sammy, our mother, and I were able to obtain a list of housing from the main office of the college. We looked at a few rentals, and I began to panic because the rentals were pretty disgusting. We ran quickly out of a few, hardly taking a look, Sammy in tow. Sammy got so discouraged that he began to lobby our mother to take me out of western Maryland. Our home was always so spotless, so pristine, and so odorless that it was hard to imagine residing in a dirty home.

Our last stop was a tall, white row house listed as 517. To our surprise, it was clean, neat, and tidy on the outside, so the three of us walked up to the painted porch with its hanging baskets and knocked on the door. We were greeted by a little, freckled-faced girl named Missy, who appeared to be about twelve years old. She looked at us, welcomed us in, and showed us the home. The home was lovely. It had a welcoming entrance and a large dining room and kitchen. Our mother noticed nursing school pictures on the walls and inquired whether Missy's mother was a nurse. Missy replied that she was. There was a third level with two bedrooms and one bathroom for two college students. It had excellent privacy, and I felt as if really good karma had brought me there. I immediately chose the front room with a beautiful window and was relieved to see a home that I could feel comfortable in. Missy took our name and phone number, promising to rent the room to us.

We drove home, and I was bursting with excitement over the room we'd found. Mostly, I was excited about the prospect of getting away from our house.

Almost as soon as we walked in the door, the phone rang. When our mother answered, the caller announced herself as Dorothy Huff, the owner of the home on 517. "I hate to tell you this," Dorothy said, "but I simply cannot rent this bedroom to your daughter because I have not met her."

Our mother grimaced and quickly responded to Dorothy's concerns. She mentioned that she too was a nurse and urged Dorothy to quickly reconsider her stand. When Dorothy was hesitant, our mother became incensed and spoke firmly to Dorothy. "You will love my daughter," she said. "She was president of the National Honor Society, a Junior Miss, and a straight A student. Consider this room rented. We will be there when school starts. Your first check and the security deposit are already in the mail. If we have any questions, we will call you. Good-bye."

I am sure Dorothy took her phone and just stared at it. Our mother always started any relationship with the superior position. Dorothy got demoted. Her opinion meant nothing. Dorothy was to do what our mother told her to do. Dorothy never forgot their first conversation, and she would repeat it several times while we were eating.

For some reason, Dorothy assented to renting the room to me, and I was introduced to her when my father brought my furniture into her home for my first experience living apart from the family. Dorothy was friendly and warm and her disposition was so great that I slept like a kitten on my first night. She prepared my bed linens with a beautiful, white quilt and lots of fluffy pillows. She put some flowers in a vase with a little note that said, "Welcome to our home."

As I lay in my bed, I thanked God for finding this home, for finding Dorothy, and for allowing me to distance myself from our mother. I cried for a bit, thinking about how brutal our mother had been to all of us. I thought about Tricia's beatings and how she had simply never given in. I thought about how her academic career had been cut short because she had been desperate to vacate our home. I thought about how she should be the one in college, joining a sorority, and dating cute boys. I cried for my siblings who were left behind. I hoped that I would eventually have a normal life and a normal husband. I cried for Paul Wayne. I cried for my mementos and my trophies, and I cried because I did not want to go home but I realized that I was not emancipated or in a position to support myself.

———•———

NOT ONLY DID I LIKE the college program, I loved the students and the instructors. I became very fond of the gentleman who started our dental program, Dr. William Fridinger, and very fond of two of the instructors, Mary Jewel Hidey and Tricia Carpenter. I felt like a bird soaring in the right direction. I felt a sense of positivity around me. I felt balance. I felt joy. It was the first time in my life that I had no bruises on my body, the first time I was free from the fear of a swinging fist coming at me. It was an oasis from the trauma that came with living in our home.

Dorothy Huff was a nurse at the local hospital and was raising two teenage children. Her husband had arbitrarily left her, so for additional income, she rented the two bedrooms on the upper level. Dorothy was employed at Sacred Heart Hospital as a nurse, and she also taught in the cardiac wing. She took her status as a heart instructor seriously and routinely prepared for the classes in her kitchen.

She was also Catholic, and I would join her on Sundays for Mass. Her Sundays were not like ours. She sang in the kitchen and made a huge breakfast. And she, Missy, David (her son), and I ate to our hearts' delight and then trotted off to church. There was no screaming. There was no hitting and no verbal assaults. It was a pleasant, happy, and pleasurable experience. It was also the first time I fully enjoyed a Church service.

Dorothy worked the night shift, and when she would return home and see my light on as I would be up studying, she would come up to see me and say, "Want some squash pie and root beer?"

So while she sat in her kitchen wearing her white, starched nurses' uniform, we would eat entire squash pies and drink tons of root beer.

She had such a funny personality. She explained that, one Easter, as she was removing the Easter turkey from the oven and she asked Missy to go get Mr. Huff, her husband. Missy told her mother that her father had instructed her to tell her mother that he was leaving forever. Literally, as Dorothy was preparing for Easter dinner, her husband was preparing to abandon the family. Somehow, she'd learned to laugh about it.

Dorothy was a sweetheart. One day, when I arrived home and walked up to the top floor, I saw a wrapped gift on my bed. I opened the card, and it said, "I thought you would like this. I see you working so hard and getting good grades. Love, Dorothy."

I cried before I opened the gift. I just sat on my bed and wept. I was receiving maternal love from this woman, and I simply appreciated the kindness and thoughtfulness. I wiped my tears and opened the gift. Dorothy had purchased white, onion skin paper for letter writing and added my initials in the corners of every page. She had an easel on the second level near a bright window, and she told me that she created diplomas for the area schools and colleges for extra money. Her work was beautiful.

As I stroked the paper, I thought how I'd longed for my own mother to draft a simple card with those words of encouragement. Not once had I received a note or a card or affirmative words that my straight A's were the result of hard work or that my awards were something to be proud of. I received no cheers when I won academic accolades or beauty pageant titles or baton trophies. Not a word. Our mother had never even enunciated the words, *I love you.*

I washed my face and quietly walked down the steps to the kitchen and just hugged Dorothy for the gesture. It was a touching moment. I loved her. I respected her. As with Paul's home, I never wanted to leave hers.

Dorothy had some run-ins with our mother. She felt that our mother was rude and disruptive to our harmony, and Dorothy hated it when she called. Dorothy became very protective of me because she now cared for me. On a few occasions, our mother called and Dorothy begrudgingly gave me the calls. Our mother was always combative.

During one conversation, our mother vented how I had nothing better to do than to study, while she was scrubbing, cleaning and cooking and that I was a miserable, unappreciative bitch. I was not sure what had provoked her. I appreciated everything that came my way. I never took anything for granted. I paid for my own tuition but did not have enough money to pay for the bedroom rental. It was hard to please our mother. One could never jump high enough or perform strongly enough.

Dorothy could overhear the conversations I had with our mother. She was quite concerned about her temperament and mental health. Years later, Dorothy told me that, several times, she had simply crossed her fingers and lied to our mother, saying I was at the college library when, in fact, I was upstairs with my head in the books. Dorothy was well aware that our mother offended me needlessly. Dorothy did not like it and did her best to prevent me from hearing it. When our mother called, Dorothy would say, "Your mother is calling to speak to the target child."

Since our mother was complaining about money all the time, I rescheduled my second semester classes so that I had full lecture days on Monday, Tuesday, Wednesday, and Thursday and drove two and a half hours to work not far from my home. On Thursdays, I would complete my classes and then hop in the car and drive straight to Tasker Middle School or Bowie Senior High School and teach baton lessons to the Belle Aire Majorettes. This work brought in a good income, and I would have spending money while away from home. I thought maybe our mother would stop complaining and settle down if I brought in more money. It was an exhausting effort because I worked on Saturday and Sunday and drove back to Cumberland late Sunday night. Dorothy was concerned with the pace and feared I would die of exhaustion. I explained to her that it was needed, that it would get our mother to stop cursing me for the added expense of extra housing.

I studied hard and loved it. Because I thought my biology instructor was handsome, I made it a point to get the highest grade on every exam. He knew that I was the top student because, after every exam, he handed the exams back in rank order, with the lowest scoring student receiving his or her test results first and the highest grader, last. I made a point that the last person would be me. Out of four tests and ten quizzes, I got my exam or quiz back last every time. I aimed to please him, and I had a huge crush on him, until I saw him kissing another instructor and walking her to her car. I also saw him holding a snake, so I stopped my crush immediately but still kept my number one class standing.

Since our mother had only enrolled me in a one-year program at Allegany due to the costs, I transferred to a two-year dental hygiene program in Baltimore, which was not as inviting and warm as Allegany had been. I became depressed at the notion of going back to the mayhem of my home and living there while attending school in Baltimore. I was so rejuvenated from the warmth of Dorothy's home, and I felt like I was moving back into hell. Our mother kept repeating that it was too expensive for me to attend a school away from home, so there was little I could do but comply. I wanted my education badly. I wanted a way to live on my own. I had the smallest thought that maybe, just maybe, it was more pleasant at home—that things might have changed for the better while I was gone. I was wrong.

I TRIED DESPERATELY TO CLOSE myself off, working and studying and generally staying out of our mother's way. There was still yelling and some hitting that got in the way of my concentration, but I demanded from myself that I would persevere. I hated the time I lost when arguments ensued in the house. Our mother was such a nut. She yelled at the slightest of things. And the chaos and dysfunction of our mother's home—her erratic behavior and mean temper—seemed even more pronounced in comparison with the calm kindness of Dorothy and her home. My poor siblings and I got a very raw deal with her. She was abnormal to say the least.

While I was enrolled in the dental hygiene program, I still had my heart set on becoming a dentist. So one day when my father was not working due to an injury, we arranged to visit the dental school. I was almost done with the two-year dental hygiene program and felt like I could handle the challenge of dental school. My father and I met with the dean, and he insisted that I sit in on a lecture. So I chose a pathology lecture.

During the lecture, my father kept leaning over to me and asking if I knew what the presentation slides depicted. Yes, I did. One slide showed Dilantin hyperplasia. Another slide showed dens en dente. Another slide showed an apthous ulcer. Then something awful was shown on the screen—a slide of a naked woman. Then came another naked, sexy woman. And another. In between the dental slides were pornographic pictures.

When the lecture was over, I was literally shaking. There were only one or two women in the class, and I noticed they sat in the back far away from the others. I marched up to the professor and candidly asked, "Why do you show those naked pictures in between the dental slides?"

His reply was "To keep the men awake."

On the way home, neither my father nor I spoke. I broke the ice and asked him, "Dad, did you like the lecture?"

He replied, "I loved it!"

Because of those slides I decided to refrain from submitting an application to dental school. I also knew that I could not handle another four years with our mother. Continuing to live with her would be unhealthy and detrimental to my overall well-being. As we drove home, I was sad. Again I felt that something wonderful was not to be because of the mental instability of our mother. The gift of becoming a dentist was within my reach but torn from my aspirations because of the lunatic in the house.

Lunatic. Nutcase. Abuser. Those words described what we lived with. Because of her, my lovely, smart sister Tricia was forced to take the first exit ramp out of the trauma of our household. She deserved more. I deserved more. My father deserved more. My siblings deserved more.

———•———

I FOCUSED ON FINDING A way to get out of my house. Finally, I resolved that if I could pass the national dental hygiene exam, the income I would make working as a hygienist would not be bad income. I could afford a place of my own and manage my own existence.

For years, I regretted not having the opportunity to attend dental school. I simply could not survive more time in the presence of our mother's anger. For years, I beat myself up, thinking of myself as a failure. But I came to realize that changing my plans and forgoing dental school was a means of survival. I would have to retrieve my repressed memories of abuse to remind myself why I did not persevere academically. I forgave myself. It was not my fault. I was the dutiful, ambitious daughter living with a monster who treated us worse than one would treat animals. Ultimately, I forgave myself for giving up plans to become a dentist. It was not in my cards. First and foremost, I needed to get out of our mother's house. I resented her for preventing me from going to dental school. If she had been a happier person, I would have pursued this course of education. I would have been able to attend dental school and reside in the home. But since she was such a nightmare, staying in the home was not an option. I'd had enough of her conduct.

Chapter Sixteen

———◆———

Destructive Events and Poor Decisions

WHILE I WAS COMPLETING MY last year of dental hygiene school, another event occurred that caused me to alter my life forever. One of the jockeys who rode with my father frequented our home and was a much loved visitor. "BV" was a tiny Italian with a lot of energy. We trusted him in our home. He and his wife began to inquire whether any of us could babysit their three young children. The riders knew we were perfect choices to protect and nurture their children. As teenagers we were good, studious, straitlaced kids. My father brought my sister, who I will not identify, to BV's home to babysit for he and his wife. Like many other racetrack families, BV was a constant presence in our household, along with his sweet wife and three young daughters.

The camaraderie between the agents, trainers, owners, and jockeys was a huge part of the industry, and most of it occurred in our kitchen. We were attractive, and we had great stories. Those who came to the house usually left feeling good or at least well fed. With their presence, our mother was on her best behavior. We would see laughter and cheer. We embraced the flow of company.

My sister who was chosen to babysit was young, shy and quiet. She was not outgoing, and she was not ambitious. She was steady and consistent but not expressive. We would always tease her and tell her that our mother accidentally brought home the wrong baby because she did not act like or resemble us. Dad agreed that she had no resemblance to the family and recalled a story in the hospital when she was born. Even the hospital staff began to question who she'd come from.

BV was in his late twenties and worked side by side with my father. They raced at the same tracks. They looked after one another during a race and tried desperately to make it around the oval safely. The other riders were a bit jealous of their friendship because all of them had tried to get close to my father and BV had been successful.

Many times, BV would repeat a story about my father having saved another rider's life during a race. Apparently, while coming down the backstretch before the clubhouse turn, a young rider was about to fall from his mount when my father quickly reached over, grabbed him with one hand, and put him back in his saddle. The maneuver cost my father the win, and he was brought before the racing stewards to explain why he had not fully ridden his horse. During the inquiry, my father firmly told the racing stewards that it was better to see that a young man avoid paralysis than to watch him fall. Dad said that he would give up a smile in a winners' circle picture to prevent that type of accident.

Watching out for others, putting others' well-being ahead of his own—that was what Dad was known for. If anyone asked my father for a favor, my father would go the extra mile to help him or her out. When one jockey left his home and abandoned his children, his wife approached Dad for some help. She was worried sick about losing her home. Dad obtained the deed to their Bowie home, brought along a notary, and asked the jockey to join him in the track kitchen for coffee and eggs. While there, Dad proceeded to talk about family and taking care of the children. As he spoke, he removed the deed to the jockey's home from his pocket and gently persuaded him to sign the deed over to his soon-to-be ex-wife. That is what Dad did. He did the right thing. He made sure people were safe. I think the jockey was too scared and too respectful of my father to say no.

When BV called upon my father for babysitting assistance, Dad stepped right in. We knew this young couple and their children. BV married his wife because, at age fifteen, she became pregnant with their first child. Even though they had made an unanticipated move toward an early pregnancy, they appeared to love each other and adored their growing family. This particular jockey was one of the "heavers." He would eat and then put his fingers down his throat to throw up. It was well known in the jocks room that he was the best at training his body how to throw up on demand. Therefore, he ate a lot and threw up a lot. At one point, he too succumbed to becoming one of my dental hygiene patients. He had practically no enamel on his teeth due to chronic heaving, so I thought the instructors would find his mouth pretty interesting.

On the day that he agreed to be one of my patients, BV insisted on picking me up in his van to drive both of us to the dental hygiene clinic. The van was sort of ridiculous and childish looking. A cartoonlike drawing of a jockey on a horse was emblazoned on the back of his van above the bumper, and inside, he kept little toys and magazines that were designed for teenagers, not an adult. I had never been alone with him prior to this drive. Routinely, we had always been surrounded by many people whenever we were together, so being alone and having a one-on-one conversation felt funny.

During the drive to Baltimore, he made comments that made me feel very, very uncomfortable. He mentioned unkind things about his marriage, which I felt I should not be privy to, especially since I liked his wife. His sharing those details of their personal life felt like a total breach to me. He mentioned that if he was single, he would like to date either my sister or me. He continued telling me intimacies and throwing suggestive comments my way. I was mortified, since I thought of him as nothing less than a married family man who worked with my father. He was way, way, way out of bounds.

After I cleaned BV's teeth, he drove his van into the parking lot of Sid Mandel's Deli not far from the Northern Parkway. I justified the stop in my mind; he was hungry, and then he would throw up in the men's room, I told myself. I made a point of eating quickly to hasten the time with him. I never spoke to anyone about the uneasy feeling I had in his presence, and I kept the conversation about his "bad" marriage private out of respect for his wife, whom I adored. I also gave him nothing to hold his head on. I had no commentary for him. I did not add to the conversation or sympathize with him.

When my first dental hygiene year ended in 1977, the summer began, and the state of flux began with the whole family traveling between Maryland, Delaware, and New Jersey, where my father rode. BV and his family continued to come to our home to hang out and to eat. I purposefully avoided him, and his presence now chilled me.

One evening, I overheard our mother making plans to take BV's wife and her three children to Hampton Beach, New Hampshire, for some fun. BV was strongly encouraging his wife to go, clearly desirous that the plans would come to fruition. Our mother, BV's wife, and their three children drove to the beach, leaving BV alone. My father was working in Delaware. My one sister and I lingered behind in our Maryland home, as we both had summer job commitments. It would be fun staying there, just her and me. But I was hoping BV would stay away, since our father was not home.

The next day, my sister asked me if I would go out with a jockey named Richard for the day. I told her emphatically no, that I did not want to go anywhere with him. I did not want anyone to see us together and conclude that we were dating. He was not my type. My sister said that she didn't want to go with him either, but he was downstairs in our home, and she didn't know what to do. Nor did she want to hurt his feelings too badly. I was not happy, but I relented.

While driving in the car with Richard, I felt gross. I did not like him. He turned to me and said, "Well, your sister didn't want to come with me because of her affair with BV, right?"

What? I literally stood up and defended my sister. I even went so far as to defend BV.

Richard said, "Tracey, everyone knows about it except your parents."

I asked Richard to take me home, and I immediately went up to my sister's bedroom and demanded to know what was going on. She denied the affair, but I pushed. "You are too young," I told her. "He is married. Our mother and dad will die, and our mother will beat you to death."

A few weeks later, the news was out. BV's wife found a love letter to my sister in her husband's van and brought it over to our house. A new nightmare began. My sister did not get beaten, but my father did try to take a baseball bat to BV. My father was fiercely angry, especially at the deception taking place under our noses and BV taking advantage of my sister. My father was also angry at BV's disrespect for his wife and disrespect for our hospitality and family. BV had definitely crossed many boundaries. The situation was not good.

You just didn't disrespect another rider or one of his cherished children, especially one so young. Since my father was the most revered rider in the jock's room, it took balls for BV to do this to him. In addition, BV knew, as would any rider, that a rider who'd disrespected another rider like that faced possible retaliation (and serious physical harm) on the track. An angry rider could deal out retribution against another rider by "dropping" him or wedging him in or cutting him off during a race. There were scores to be settled, and riders were the judge and jury. It was the way. You just did not harm another rider or a member of their family.

Even though BV's wife blamed my sister and her husband equally, the affair was his orchestration. My sister was just a young child, not mature enough to decipher between love and a married man's urge to get sex outside his marriage. It was discovered that the affair started when my sister was babysitting his three small children and BV's wife was away visiting her family. It began sometime after our ride to the dental hygiene clinic that day. I regretted not warning my sister to be leery of him. If our mother was a normal person, I would definitely have informed her of his advances. I was riddled with guilt because I knew this sister would not have known what to do with the attention from him. She would have been like a bee stuck in honey. Trapped.

We never thought to go to the authorities back then. BV was never penalized, but we certainly were. After the affair was discovered, our mother's anger resurged and became a newer version that I can describe only as high octane insanity. To her, the affair put another blemish on the family and stigmatized her as a less than perfect mother. People were whispering, and rumors about BV and my sister began to flow. The younger siblings felt our mother's wrath too. She exploded at the smallest disruption and began to also yell at visiting children, who would run for cover.

In my parents' defense, how can any parent handle a situation like that? It was the only time I gave our mother a hall pass to freak out. It was an intolerable situation for any family, not just ours, to deal with. The incident has a name—statutory rape.

Traumatized, my sister became emotionally dependent on our mother, her mannerisms and interactions with the world became somewhat infantile, and she never left our mother's side her entire adult life. Our mother did not retaliate against my sister. My sister never got beaten for her affair with BV. She was fragile—a perfect choice for a sexual predator and a perfect choice for an unyielding mother to control.

I could see this dynamic between mother and daughter and wanted none of it. She was not going to control me into adulthood. It was sick and twisted. It was a weird symbiotic relationship. I would rather clean my house with my tongue than succumb to that.

This sister never weaned from our mother. Maybe it was the "queen bee" syndrome. It is better to align with the mean queen bee than to be treated abusively by the queen. They became conjoined for another forty years.

Chapter Seventeen

Exit Ramp

IT WAS 1977, AND I contemplated my goals once more. It dawned on me that I should have been enjoying the best time of my life. Instead, I was trying to cope with the dynamics of my own home. I was twenty years old. I never drank. I didn't use any drugs. I didn't smoke. I didn't go party. I was studious. I was straitlaced. I was also trapped.

I needed to make decisions. The decisions of an abuse victim are often not good ones. They are survival based. You become like an animal caught in a trap. You just do what you have to do to get out. Although my mind was riddled with bad memories and the cumulative effect of trauma, my body was healthy. I had boundless energy, and that energy would take me to the place I needed to be. I knew if I applied and was accepted to another dental school, one free of nudie slides, I would remain trapped in an untenable situation. I was fairly certain I could not withstand another four years of residing in our mother's home; it would surely do me in. Five other children lived in the home still, and the drama and yelling occurred daily. I did not want more memories of this abode.

I began to feel like I deserved an opportunity to excel. Families should give ambitious children a venue to strive. Our mother thwarted all of our potential successes. She was a hindrance. She was in the way. Her mental health affected us deeply. Instead of living in a peaceful domicile that allowed us to focus on achieving our potential, we were stuck in this terrible place and all we could focus on was finding an exit ramp out of there. We needed to remove ourselves from the fear of living.

So I started dating and got out via a courthouse marriage. It was necessary. Was I insanely in love? No. Was I using my new beau as an escape ramp? Yes. Was he a good person? Yes. Was I alive and hopeful? Yes.

IN AN ACT OF SHEER defiance, I had the audacity to leave our mother a note in the mailbox informing her that, by the time she read the note, I would be married and driving far away. Kitty Carson told me that our mother went nuts, cursing me and screaming her head off, when she found my note in the mailbox. The good thing is that I was nowhere she could reach me to strike my face or body. It gave me satisfaction to know that I had finally hurt her, even though it was not physically. I had basically flipped her the bird. In fact, to make sure I was far enough away, my new husband and I drove to Canada.

I was free! Now the beast of a mother had to come up with a perfect explanation to her circle of friends as to why her bright, ambitious second daughter ran out of the home. God knows what she told them.

Running off to get married was my only act of defiance, and I owe the man I married a huge apology for not being truthful with him.

I just jumped on the boat to save myself. I also thought, because I did care for this young man, that I could possibly make it work. We cared for each other, but the caring was not deep enough to sustain a lifetime together. Our mother made it a point to curse the union. She constantly criticized my young spouse, and she prayed for the marriage to fail in order to prove a point—that my conduct was wrong.

———•———

IN 1979, ALMOST TWO YEARS had passed during which I did not speak to our mother. Kitty sat me down and told me that life would improve if there was an olive branch between our mother and me. So, slowly, a discussion began. I cannot explain why I reached out to her any more than I can explain why the boy who was abused told his foster mother that he missed his mother. Although I did not miss our mother, I missed the goings on of my siblings who were still at home. During the silent period, our mother refused to allow me to contact them.

Then I got a bit of an upper hand with our mother. I had introduced Mitzy to her future husband. Our mother was pleased since Mitzy seemed so lonely. Our mother wanted to keep tabs on that relationship, and the best way to do that was to reconnect with me. Plus, I was pregnant with the first family grandchild. So in exchange for being allowed to stay close to my siblings, I agreed to reconnect with our mother.

My spouse and I had purchased the most adorable townhome and hired a decorator to decorate it. When our mother came into the home, she was totally surprised at how beautiful it was. I did not want her to enter my home, but I thought about how the roles had reversed. This was my home, and I could do whatever with whomever I wanted. If she got out of control, I could order her to leave. Her reaction to my home—a mixture of amazement and shock—was odd; she seemed disbelieving that we could put such a tasteful home together. She also appeared to be jealous of the home and demanded to know who the decorator was. She did not like to be trumped. I had trumped her, and it made her uncomfortable. She made *me* uncomfortable. I hated her down deep. I was just going through the motions allowing her presence in my home.

My siblings were thrilled that a baby was on the way and could not get enough of watching the nursery wallpapering and furniture delivery. Robby assisted in putting the crib together, and there was a fresh delight in the air. Buddy was lighting holy candles to assure a boy would fill the crib.

My son was born at Washington Hospital Center on April 20, 1980, at 10:01 p.m. He came into the world at seven pounds six ounces. Like a good little race tracker, he chose to be born on a day when the track was closed. After a twenty-four-hour labor, while watching Howard Cosell on television all day, I finally delivered my child. When he popped out, I started to laugh because he looked exactly like Buddy.

My family was attending a sports dinner in Baltimore, and Robby called my spouse and was filled in on the news that a new little boy was now part of the family. I cuddled my newborn and vowed that he would never feel the fear of physical abuse or the bite of words that would damage his little ego. I held him tightly and told him that he would be cherished, protected, and safe. I would kiss him forever.

In 1980, mothers remained in the hospital after giving birth much longer than they do today. I ended up contracting a slight fever and an infection, so my stay was extended to a week. During the week, our mother did not visit me or see my son. My sisters encouraged her to go see her first grandchild and to check on me, but our mother's reply was "I do not like babies."

I guess either out of sheer guilt or pressure from her friends and my siblings, she showed up the day I was packing my suitcase to come home. I immediately felt the need to keep her away from my baby. I felt that she was not welcome to hold him, even though she did. I became super protective of him and felt like the devil was touching him.

———◆———

MY SON EXPERIENCED COLIC, AND he constantly cried during his first year. Nothing seemed to console him. My hair fell out. All of my hair on my body fell out. I shrunk down to about ninety-six pounds. I could not ask our mother what to do, so I visited the pediatrician who had been my pediatrician while I was growing up.

Dr. Fietel knew my entire family. He was not the same pediatrician who'd advised our mother to beat Tricia within an inch of her life. I cannot remember when Dr. Fietel actually became the family pediatrician, but he was always mine. He was the local doctor who took care of us. He always accepted our mother's explanations for our bruises over the years. She would say that we played a lot in the woods, that we often fell off our bikes, that we fell off the trampoline, that the dog dragged us along the yard, or that our batons had damaged our skin. Dr. Fietel never questioned her. I chose him to be my new baby's pediatrician because I'd always believed he had a warm heart.

So on a visit to him, I explained that my son cried continuously, and I could not seem to get him to stop.

"To get rid of the crying, send this child to your mother," Doctor Fietel advised. "She will get him to stop crying."

I darted a glance at him and replied, "I want him to stop crying, not learn how to salute." I did not tell Dr. Fietel that I did not trust our mother.

When my son was one month old, our mother somehow convinced me to drive with her to Hampton Beach. I agreed because I was having a bit of trouble with my spouse's need to smoke marijuana every day. I balanced the trauma of being with her with the fun I would have walking on the boardwalk with my newborn and eating fried clams and seeing my wonderful grandmother and Aunt Marilyn.

I sat in the front passenger seat while our mother drove. A console separated us. My son was crying incessantly, but it was not an ear-piercing cry, just a continuous cry from a one month old. I nursed him, but he still was uneasy. I cuddled him and kissed him, and he still remained restless. During that time, very few individuals utilized car seats or seat belts. As children, we simply frolicked about on the inside of our automobiles. As adults, we found the seatbelts to be uncomfortable and seldom used them. How we never got injured, I will never know. Our mother told me to place my four-week old child on the console and rub his back.

While I rubbed his back, our mother lifted her arm and said, "This will shut him up." And she slammed her hand down so hard that my son's feet and hands stretched out from the impact. My son instantly became quiet. Then she said, "Well, that shut him up, didn't it?" She was proud of her actions. What a maniac she was. I was totally shocked. I was numb. I was absolutely disgusted. Then I got scared.

My son did not make a move during the entire nine-hour drive after our mother hit him. When we arrived at the beach, he was still in a heavy sleep, so I prepared the small crib I'd brought for him and placed him in it. On reflection, I think he was probably unconscious. He was breathing but not moving. After a few more hours, I heard a tiny little whimper. Luckily, he was back in action. Yet he remained lethargic for the rest of the evening. He was pretty calm all night and breast-fed quietly.

I tiptoed around our mother so as not to get her revved up. I desperately wanted to enjoy some sun and surf. I had looked very pale since my son was born, so I was hoping to work on my tan when he was asleep.

Our mother rented the same oceanfront apartment year after year. Historically, when all of us were loaded in the station wagon, gleeful of our arrival at the beach, our mother would insist that we not enter the apartment for hours until she had completely cleaned it. We would, of course, all want to use the bathroom after a long ride, but she would insist that we pee outside. She cursed the landlord, cursed the previous occupant, cursed us for being hungry, and cursed our father for not being present to assist her. She was one frustrated vacationer. She always set the tone for a bumpy vacation.

Never did a day go by that she did not feel overwhelmed. The bar height she made for herself often seemed impossible to achieve. Most of the time she was her own worst enemy. Perfection was what she reached for. The work to get there was too arduous a task and only led to frustration and anxiety. Our mother could simply not put the bar lower.

On this visit to Hampton Beach, our mother started to get irritated. She was not happy that the baby was crying. She was not happy that I could not soothe him. At one point, she came into my bedroom and lunged to grab me but I frenetically walked a few feet away, leaving the crib between us.

"So, you are so smart," she snarled at me. "What the hell are you going to do with that miserable husband of yours?"

"Well, we have a baby so we are going to try to work on it," I retorted.

Then a cunning expression spread across her face. "You are so stupid," she said, her tone filled with contempt. "You don't even know that pot plants are growing in your backyard."

Pot plants in my backyard? I had not really looked at my backyard since the baby was born. There was not too much to look at; it was a small townhouse backyard.

She continued to taunt me in a pompous manner by saying, "If you think that your marriage was made in heaven, you better rethink it. You will never survive. You will be a single parent with no money. You will probably lose your child if he fights you."

I'd had enough. She could not hit me, but that tongue was a powerful weapon in her arsenal. I shook the crib as if to push it in her direction. It was the closest I ever got to actually striking her. I decided to go back home, resolving that this little vacation had been a huge mistake. I located a payphone and phoned my dear New England friend Phil and asked him if he would take me to the airport for a flight home.

A FEW MONTHS AFTER THE beach trip, an article in the newspaper caught my eye. It told the story of a babysitter who had shaken a baby in her care so hard that the child had died. The image of our mother striking my very fragile infant flashed through my mind. Today, of course, we are very aware of shaken baby syndrome and of how it can lead to the death of society's most fragile members. I cursed our mother and vowed that if she ever struck me or my child again, I would pick up a kitchen knife and kill her. I fantasized about it. I wanted her to lash out at us one more time. I would have no remorse watching her bleed to death.

And if that did not happen—if she died a normal death due to old age—I would take a small knife and insert it under her blouse as she lay in her coffin, pushing it into her dead flesh. It would make me smile, thinking she was dead inside the coffin with a perpetual knife lodged in her side. I dreamed of laying flowers on her grave, spitting on the ground above her, and smiling, knowing a knife inserted by me, her second child, was stuck in her side. The action would be a sweet revenge.

God must have been watching over her. It would be thirty years before she hit me again. I still hang on to the little knife, waiting to get the news that she is dead. I pray that Maryland never gets a desecration of dead body statute.

In 1982, my spouse felt that returning to Canada was the best path for him. After many attempts to keep our marriage together, we both gave in. Concerned about money, the first thought was that I could sell the beautiful baby items I had acquired. I could use the money on a down payment on a temporary rental for myself and my baby. My brothers took two highchairs, two strollers, two playpens, a bassinet, two swings, and a crib and placed them in the corner of my parents' unfinished basement. It made me ill that the items were in that home, but I could not afford to place the items in storage. I had Robby take me to the big house to retrieve the items.

When we drove up to the house, I began to shudder. I hated looking at it. It was a nice home, but the events that had occurred inside the home made me sick to my stomach.

"Robby, I don't want to go in there," I said. "Can I just help you when you drag the pieces outside?"

"Tracey, no one's home," Robby said. "Come in. We can be quick."

When we got down to the basement, I saw nothing. I asked Robby if he knew what had happened to my belongings, and he said he had no idea. While we were standing there, I heard footsteps coming down the basement stairs. I recognized those footprints as the black cloud coming. I looked over and saw the beast. I stared at her. "Do you know what happened to the baby things that were left in the basement?" I asked.

"The baby things?" she replied. "Oh I gave them to Terri Fieldstone to help her out because she has no money."

It was my baton trophies and mementos all over again. "Those were my things," I said. "I need to sell those things for a down payment on a rental."

She looked at me and said, "Well, I don't know what to tell you. I guess you will have to get a second job if you need the money."

I could have predicted this. I never should have left my belongings in that house. I simply forgot about her habit of giving our things away. "You could have asked me before you did that," I said. "I should have been the one to say yes or no to Terry Fieldstone.

"

"Why don't you shut your fucking mouth up and go home," she spat back. "Do not disrespect me."

Respect her? I loathed her. She did not deserve respect. This was another example of her disregard for her child's desires or wishes for the sake of impressing others. Memories flooded my brain, and I felt like I could not breathe.

My brother took me by my arm and gently walked me out of the house. He felt bad for me. "I am sorry, Tracey," he said. "I am so sorry."

I looked at my sweet brother and took his right hand in mine as he drove away from the torture chamber of a home we'd grown up in. "She needs to die, Robby. Why is she still alive? She makes me ill. Let's get out of here. I hate looking at her, and I hate looking at this house," I said. "I will not feel totally free until I see her in the ground. I do not know why I try to have a relationship with her. Every time I try, I get disappointed. It is all such a reach for her. She is so cold. She has no idea how injured we are because of her."

CHAPTER EIGHTEEN

---◆---

THE POWER OF FRIENDSHIP

SADLY, MY MARRIAGE ENDED IN divorce. I proceeded to carve out a life for myself and my son. We were fortunate enough to rent a basement apartment in the home of an older jockey. We felt safe, and my son loved swimming in the pool in the backyard. I continued to work as a dental hygienist, and my father was a great help in watching my son if I got stuck working late. I had very little contact with our mother during this time, but I knew she was with my child when my father would take him to play in the yard that had been part of my childhood home. I always questioned my son when he arrived home to me. I did not want our mother laying a finger on him.

I worried about money all the time. Kitty Carson had some thoughts on that matter. While I was cleaning the teeth of a patient one day, Kitty literally strolled into the room and interrupted me. I was seated on my dental stool, wearing my gloves and mask, and Kitty said, "Tracey Mary, you are leaving this profession and coming to work with me at my new office. I just opened a new real estate company, and I need agents. And you need money, so call me when you are done today. Say good-bye to this godforsaken job."

I looked up from my startled patient and replied, "Why on earth would I want to sell dirty, old homes?"

Kitty laughed and said, "Why on earth would you clean dirty, old teeth?"

My patient was getting upset, and I told Kitty that I would call her in the evening.

Before I knew it, Kitty had me enrolled in a class to obtain my real estate license and taunted me with the thought of huge commissions. Once I'd passed the test, I began selling real estate at night after my dental hygiene workday. Once I got enough commissions on the books and felt comfortable with leaving dental hygiene, I would stop.

Kitty always looked out for me. She was the second most important person in my life, and I loved her unconditionally. Forever, she was a breath of fresh air and gave me a song in my heart. She made me laugh with her stories of smoking pot in the 1960s and how she'd literally one day burned her bra and began a career in real estate.

Aside from Kitty, the one person who was the most integral person in my life was my best friend, Janet Turcotte. She was the sister-in-law of Ron Turcotte, the jockey riding Secretariat when Secretariat won the Triple Crown. Janet was also divorced from a Canadian jockey, and she had two small daughters. I'd met Janet briefly when I was nineteen years old while waiting at the racetrack for Sammy to complete his work day. She was very sweet with a wicked sense of humor. We had a lot of things in common besides children and racing. She was also a dental hygienist, although she'd let her license lapse to raise her children.

One day, Janet reached out to me and asked if I could spend some time with her in my dental office and refresh her on taking x-rays and the use of the newest equipment. We also set a time to drive down to the dental school and set up slides to refresh her memory so she could retake the hygiene test.

During this time, we became closer, and that friendship lasted until the day she died. There was not a day that went by that we did not start and end our days by talking on the phone. We were connected in a way that had a huge impact on my well-being.

Having Janet's friendship was like having a permanent therapist at my beck and call. She knew my family and the dynamics and when I would complain or moan, she had a great knack for targeting the issue and resolving it in a way that brought me back to the right path. She was a great listener too. We developed a deep love and respect for one another as we raised our children and took beautiful vacations together. I trusted Janet completely and felt secure in the fact that, whatever deeply rooted feelings or thoughts I conveyed to her, those feelings and thoughts would not be judged or dismissed. Janet had the raw end of the deal because she was so easily satisfied. I was the opposite. I was always searching, always dreaming. Janet somehow contained my aspirations in the realm of reality, and I appreciated her with all my heart.

Janet and I were both extremely lonely, so I decided to check out a new, hip health club in Rockville, Maryland. Upon arriving I felt really old even though I was only twenty-seven years old. It was 1984, and the "yuppie" generation was alive and well. The club's members consisted of a diverse group of professionals, and everyone drove great-looking cars, like BMWs and Mercedes. I wanted what they had. I wanted it all.

So I returned home, called Janet, and scheduled a time to sign her up at the gym. We had two goals. One goal was to get in shape, and the other was to meet someone to date.

While touring the gym, I glanced over and saw the most gorgeous Asian man playing racquetball with a woman. I could not take my eyes off of him. Not only was he the most gorgeous Asian man I had ever seen, he was one of the most good-looking men I had ever laid my eyes on. Above the racquetball court was a restaurant with a great vantage point from which to stare, so I dragged Janet up to a table and just watched him play. I looked at Janet and said, "Look at that guy out there. Isn't he handsome?"

Janet smiled and said, "Yes, he looks like he is having fun, but he is with a girl."

"I don't care," I replied. "To me, it does not look like a love thing. It looks like they are just friends."

My attraction to this man also stemmed from his smile. He was happy, and he generated this cosmic type of positive energy. I was hooked and immediately signed up at the gym. I wrote down the day and time he was playing and vowed to return to the gym at the same time in order to bump into him again. Yep, I was going to gently stalk him.

<hr>

I COULD NOT STAND THE waiting any longer. As soon as I completed my last patient the next day, I arranged for my father to take care of my son, grabbed my gym bag, and drove to the gym. I positioned myself in the restaurant above the racquetball courts. And sure enough, he showed up. I observed him talking to his friends and then to the girl he had been with the evening before. He was smiling and joking and seemed confident but not cocky.

I followed the girl into the locker room and sat while she showered. As she was blow-drying her hair, I approached her and began a discussion. "Hi. I noticed you with a nice guy playing racquetball. Is that your boyfriend?"

She looked up at me with a grin and said, "No that is my shoe salesman. He sells shoes for a living."

He did not look like a shoe salesman, but I continued the

conversation. "Well," I said, "I wear a lot of shoes. so maybe one day I will see him in his store and buy some shoes from him."

She turned and said, "Maybe."

When I left the locker room, I could not locate the man I'd come to see, so I went ahead and drove home.

The following day, I could not stop thinking about this stranger. I just had to get close to him and surround myself with his spirit. He seemed nice. Again, I returned to the gym after work and immediately saw him. He was next to the girl from the locker room, and I saw her nudge him and point in my direction. He looked straight at me, and I tried to act like I was preoccupied, but there it was. Our first glance. I felt a shot of electricity run through my body and was intrigued by it.

I exercised, and from across the room, I could see him now and then looking at me. When I walked down to the locker room to retrieve my belongings, he followed and stopped to talk to me.

"Hi, my name is Dan," he said. "My friend Fran mentioned that you might be interested in playing some racquetball."

Racquetball? I wanted to die a quick death because I did not know how to play racquetball.

"Why yes," I said, biting my lip. "I would love to play racquetball."

"Great. Can you play tomorrow? How about six o'clock?" he asked.

Literally, at that point, I leaned against the wall and the fire detector alarm went off

And that is how my meeting with Dan began—innocently, with lots of bells and whistles.

I discovered during that racquetball game that Dan was not a shoe salesman. He proceeded to tell me that he was in his final year of medical school and that he had been accepted into an orthopedic residency. How perfect! I mentioned to him that my father was a professional athlete and had spent exhaustive hours at the orthopedist's office.

We made a date, and from there, our relationship grew and grew, and we became fond of each other. There was just one issue. I had not mentioned to Dan that I had a child. For some reason, I wanted to act like a regular twenty-five-year-old with remaining academic aspirations and not dwell on the history of a broken past. I had not been intimate with Dan, since if I was, he would find out about my son. I just wanted the relationship to be normal. I wanted to be in a spot where I should be. I also made a vow not to discuss my family's abusive past. I did not want to be labeled "damaged goods."

Janet encouraged me to fold and to finally have sex with Dan. Since I had moved from the basement rental into a new condo, I thought that Dan should finally see where I lived. I had avoided his requests to see my place for months, but now it was the time of reckoning.

When Dan arrived at my home, I opened the door and began to walk him around. My son's room was closed, and he was spending time with my father. Dan looked down the hall and asked, "So what room is that?"

I slowly took the doorknob and turned it, to reveal a room filled with boy things and toys. Dan looked around and then said, "You seem to collect a lot of stuffed animals."

I laughed and nervously said, "These things belong to my son, who is four years old."

Dan did not hesitate. "A son," he said. "Well, I accept you and your son."

If I were beginning to fall in love with Dan, that statement sealed the deal.

WE WERE PREPARING TO GET married in December 1987 when I discovered that I was pregnant. It was very unexpected, and I worried. Dan was still in school, and I was already exhausted from long real estate days. I changed the wedding date to November 7, 1987, and conspired with Father Mike at St. Mary's to indicate that Dan was indeed Catholic so that we could marry in the church.

Then it hit me. I began to feel overwhelming doubts about my relationship with Dan. I started noticing a bit of selfishness in him, and it worried me. I would need help with another child, and I could see that Dan was spending hours upon hours exercising, bike riding, water skiing, and sailing. He never helped with daily chores or did anything like pick up food.

At this juncture, Janet was vitally important, and I reached out to her to keep me steady. She reminded me that Dan would one day have a good salary and that he would make a great father. I became complicit in allowing Dan to put all of his exercising and fun-filled sports in front of me. But I always felt a void that was not sitting well with me.

I should have gone to counseling. I should have told the stories of my past to a professional and talked things through. I should have been more vocal with Dan. In fact, I shut down my feelings and my desires. I wanted a companion. Instead, I felt like I got another person to take care of. Little did he know, I was in desperate need of warmth and time and understanding. Dan kept saying that I was strong, that I was independent. I think counseling would have helped me express my feelings to Dan. Our mother never allowed us to express our feelings. Her mantra continued in my brain. Don't let them see you cry. Don't let them see you upset. My internal mantra was "Help, I need somebody. Help, not just anybody."

I went through the motions. Dan and I got married. I kept kicking my doubts to the back of my mind; after all, I was eagerly awaiting the birth of my second child. One afternoon, we decided to visit a doctor friend of Dan's to learn the gender of our baby. With my son in tow, I lay on the medical bed while the doctor navigated his instrument across my big belly, and the images appeared on a screen. With three words, we finally knew. "It's a girl."

How wonderful. A girl. A daughter to hold and love and cherish. I touched my belly and spoke to her and told her that I would use every bit of strength in my body to protect her from harm. I promised her that. I could not wait to meet her and begin loving her.

Our daughter was born on April 4, 1988, and we were overjoyed. She looked super Asian, and the medical staff kept commenting on how clear it was who the father was. Dan's elderly parents and his sister came to the hospital to meet the newest member of the family. I could not stop kissing her and talking to her. The first words I said to her were expressions of how much I would love her and how much I would adore her and how hard I would try to see that she was happy. I did not let go. She fascinated me because of the mixture of our races, as well as the immediate bond that I felt with her upon her delivery.

Once I'd settled back in my hospital room, my mind floated to contemplations of how our mother had brushed all of us aside as if we were a chore, a nuisance, instead of gravitating toward us like a mother to her cubs. Having my own daughter, I could not fathom treating her like that. The protective mode kicked in so strongly that I could not quite wrap my head around our mother's beatings of us at such a young age. How did she lose the connection? Why did she want the disconnect? How did we go from being her offspring in need of assistance to being so vilified by her?

I took in every smile that my baby made, every coo, every funny face, and every dirty diaper. I loved all of it. I cherished parenthood, and so did my siblings. They made special attempts to come rejoice with me. As my siblings had children of their own, our children would become a testament to breaking the cycle of abuse. Our children would run toward us, not hide from us. Our children would confide in us and ask for our advice, not seek the embrace and the warmth of others.

During this time, our mother tried to be a consistent presence in our home. For some reason, she was polite toward my son but immediately had disdain for my daughter. While we were all relaxing at a neighbor's pool one day when my daughter was just a few months old, our mother walked over and looked at my baby. "Such a shame," she said. "She will never look like us. Too bad."

This was the beginning of insults our mother would sling toward my daughter, and I would have none of it.

I turned to our mother. "I love the way she looks," I said. "And she will grow into a real beauty."

I decided to keep our mother away from my daughter so as not to poison my child's spirit and confidence.

My husband and I built a home. We raised our son and new daughter. We sent them to private school. We grew his medical practice. Along the way, I got pretty lost. For some reason, Dan and I immediately went our separate ways as far as activities, and when we went on family vacations, Dan would put the luggage down and leave us until it was time for dinner. It was lonely. I began to want more of a companion. I knew Dan was in love with me and cherished our child. He simply preferred to stay at the gym for hours or travel with one of the other doctors.

I felt needy but never complained. Just as I had kept my thoughts private as a child, I kept my feelings to myself. My children were growing up. I decided that, once they were old enough, I would seek a more compassionate companion.

As an abused child, you become strong but internally very needy. As I was taking care of the duties of a wife and mother, I went into a type of free fall. I again felt the need to find an exit ramp. I appeared to be the rock of my family, but I yearned for more love and affection. I wanted companionship. I wanted constant "I love yous." I wanted a consistent flow of warmth. I needed a man to circle his arms around me and embrace me and make me feel protected. I was tired of being the strong one. I was lonely.

CHAPTER NINETEEN

GOING FOR IT, JANET, AND CANCER

AS MY MARRIAGE WAS TAKING a downward turn, I decided to get a professional degree. As a young person, I had been more academically equipped than many individuals. My academic goals had taken a backseat to the goal of removing myself from our abusive household. I found it ironic that, for all the resentment our mother had toward her children, I found just as much resentment toward her for preventing me from thriving.

As I got older, my back was beginning to bother me. I knew that crouching over as I would have to if I pursued a dental career was out of the question. Tricia somehow got herself accepted to medical school in her thirties. So I began to think about applying to law school. I did not love the law enough to make that my choice. I simply loved thinking that if I attended law school, our mother would not win, and I could financially stand on my own. Acceptance into law school would prove that she had not accomplished the total destruction of me that she had apparently set out to achieve. She tried so hard to break all of us down, but somehow we rose above her many attempts to hurt us.

People ask me how this happened. How did my siblings and I rise above the pain of our abuse? I presume it was just determination— determination to succeed, determination to live peaceful lives free of physical trauma, and determination to break away from her and her conduct.

———•———

WHEN MY SON REACHED COLLEGE age and my daughter was well grounded in middle school, I decided that I would attend law school if given the opportunity. I had taken the easy way out of our mother's home with a courthouse marriage. As a result, I'd had a short marriage and a little baby. Now would be my time to prove that I could do it. I still had a lot of ambitiousness, and I wanted to fulfill my academic goals, so that I wouldn't regret not having done so later in life.

I enrolled in law classes at the University of Maryland night program to hone my concentration skills. I took classes to prepare for the law school entrance exam, the LSAT. Then I applied and was accepted to law school in 2000. I loved the entire process of obtaining a JD. I adored my fellow classmates, my instructors, and the challenge of the work. It was satisfying.

At the end of my second year, a fellow classmate, who was my age, called and asked me if I wanted to take a class pertaining to horse racing law, in Saratoga Springs, New York. She was a racetrack enthusiast and wanted me to join her on a short trip to New York.

I agreed to attend the session, and during the month of August 2001, we traveled to New York. We stayed at the lovely Gideon Putnam Hotel, the venue of the session. We also took in some sights. And I reached into the recesses of my brain, attempting to conjure some childhood memories from the time I'd spent there.

My classmate and I celebrated the grandeur of Saratoga Springs and its rich history. Saratoga Springs is home to world-class horse racing and horse sales and the location of both the National Museum of Dance and National Horse Racing Hall of Fame and Museum. The summers blossom with flowers and tourism, and the townspeople do a great job putting out the town welcome mat. Although the winters can be pretty snowy, the summers are amazing, and nearby Lake George and Lake Placid draw people from all over the world. It is a great place to raise children and to avoid the crime evident in many major areas of the country.

I had not seen Saratoga in years and was totally captivated by it now. I decided I would make plans to move there after I'd completed law school; it was there that I would begin a new chapter in my life. I would have my law degree and, if I was strong enough to proceed, a divorce decree as well. I set goals but put the divorce on the shelf until after I'd completed law school and finalized the bar exam.

So, for the next few years, I enrolled my daughter in field hockey camps sponsored by Skidmore College. She loved them and would use her newfound skills on her team at her private school in Maryland.

Every year since 2001, the summertime ritual was the same. I would load up the car, grab Janet and my daughter, and we would live it up during August in Saratoga. We would shop, tour, eat, and take in the races. There were galas to attend and new people to meet.

While eating dinner at a great restaurant one evening, Janet and I looked at each other and wondered why no men ever talked to us. My daughter spoke up. "Mom, it is because you and Janet come across as two gay women, and I look like your love child," she said. Maybe she was right. Ever since Janet and I had become best friends, we had spoken to each other every day, and we used words like *honey* and *sweetie* when we spoke to one another.

Janet and I had a great deal of respect for each other, and I can honestly say that we never spoke a cross word or had an argument. We just never had conflict. She knew each of my siblings, adored my father, and respected our mother. I thought of her as the oldest child in our family.

Born in 1950, Janet was seven years older than I was. She was a good travel companion, but because she had little money, I typically paid for her fun. She was a constant presence in my parents' home, as well as in my marital home. She had been through every life phase with me, from my elopement to my labor and deliveries to my law school graduation. She also knew horse racing because of her brother-in-law. Janet got a first-hand look at that period of horse racing history and her home was filled with Secretariat artifacts that would make any sports enthusiast happy.

IN AUGUST 2003, JANET AND I decided to attend the Racing Hall of Fame induction ceremony and have some fun in Saratoga. At the time, Janet was having some pain in her lower left pelvic area, and a CT scan indicated a pretty large ovarian cyst and some swelling of the colon. On the scan report, there was a recommendation for her to have a colonoscopy. Janet balked at that suggestion but vowed to first take care of the cyst and then advance to having her colon checked out.

At the last minute, Janet decided to have her ovarian cyst removed and forego Saratoga. She was nervous, and the night before her surgery, she and I spoke from my hotel room in Saratoga. That conversation still haunts me. She said, "Tracey, what if I have cancer?"

Cancer? I reassured her that she was only getting an ovarian cyst removed and that our mutual ob-gyn, Jed Gould, who delivered my son and one of her daughters, would take good care of her. In fact, I spoke to Jed before I left for Saratoga, asking if Janet would be okay and he said, "Go to Saratoga and have some fun for the both of you. Stop worrying. I will take good care of Janet." We were longtime patients of Jed's and trusted him implicitly. Jed liked Janet and me, and we adored his nurse, Shirley Messer.

I could not concentrate on the induction ceremony, so I went back to my hotel room. As soon as I walked into the room, I saw the red light on the room phone light up. I was aware that Janet was going into surgery at 9:30 a.m. Looking at that red light, I instantly knew that there was trouble with Janet.

I phoned my husband, and he informed me that Janet's eldest daughter, Stacey, was trying to reach me to inform me that her mom had gone into surgery and the doctor had found cancer.

I phoned Stacey and let her know I was getting in my car and driving to the hospital. Stacey was pleased to hear that I would be at Holy Cross Hospital as quickly as I possibly could. She had to get back to her small children and husband. Stacey mentioned that Janet was still sleeping and not aware of her condition. She did not know that her procedure had been more extensive than she'd expected. Not only had she undergone the cyst removal, she'd had a complete hysterectomy, and part of her colon had been excised. I quickly gathered up my things and got on the road. I wanted to be there when Janet woke up.

While driving I began to worry. I could not remember my adult life without Janet. I could not remember a vacation without Janet or a day when I didn't hear her voice. I had to make this better. I had to somehow get the cancer out of her body. I had to get her well. So as I drove, I incessantly phoned medical friends for words of wisdom. One friend, Joe Kaplan, an oncologist, told me he had privileges at Holy Cross Hospital. Hearing how nervous and distraught I was, he very generously planned on arriving at the hospital to check on Janet about the same time as my estimated time of arrival. I felt like Janet would be in good hands with Joe and that Joe would tell us the truth about her condition and not sugarcoat it. Joe's daughter, Raquel, grew up with my daughter, and Janet had met the entire Kaplan family at one of the school events. Janet was impressed with Raquel and predicated that she would be future valedictorian, so I knew Janet would approve of this new assignment for her care.

When I arrived at Holy Cross, it was hot as hell out, a typical Washington, DC, muggy day. The hospital smelled like cleaning fluids, and it was hectic and busy on every floor. I went straight to Janet's room and was relieved that I found her alone and sleeping. So I looked around, secured some of her belongings, and waited.

After two hours, Janet woke up, looked at me and asked me what I was doing in my leopard dress and why was I not in Saratoga at the inductions. I directly said, "Janet, there are issues. Dr. Gould found colon cancer and had to do a hysterectomy, and he removed part of your colon."

She looked up at me and said, "I have cancer?"

I told her that she had cancer, but we would beat it. I told her that she had staples down her belly and informed her that Joe Kaplan was coming in to talk to her. With her dry sense of humor, she said, "Joe Kaplan! I have a crush on him and he is going to see me looking like this?"

As soon as she said those words, Joe walked in. He greeted me and then reintroduced himself to Janet and slowly discussed the four levels of colon cancer. We both listened intently until Joe had finished. Janet asked him what level she was at, and he informed her that she was at stage four, the highest level. I could not believe my ears.

She looked at me and said, "You mean I am finally at the highest level of something?"

I began to laugh, but my heart was breaking. Things were not supposed to be like this. We were supposed to grow old together. We were supposed to enjoy life now that we had raised our kids, and we were supposed to gas ourselves in our car while she listened to Bobby Darin and I listened to Marvin Gaye when we were too frail to take care of ourselves. We had old age all figured out.

I looked at Janet and said, "You are messing up our future, Janet."

JANET WAS SLOW TO RECOVER. I sat with her every day, but I knew that my bar review courses were to begin soon and that I would be unavailable during the day. It seemed so unfair. We talked about her symptoms prior to the diagnosis. She'd always had trouble going to the bathroom, and my sisters remarked that they thought she looked really weak at my father's seventieth birthday party. I'd attributed Janet's tired look to age and working too much and just shrugged my sisters' assessment off. We reflected on the positive hepatitis test she'd had and the funny rash she'd developed on her arms, and we reminded ourselves that she had barely been able to get out of bed to attend my law school graduation two months earlier.

I reassured her that I would help her through this, that she would get better, and that we would start off with Joe as a treating physician and then add the best DC had to offer with a backup oncologist. I reassured her that she would survive. But I knew in my heart that this was bad; the pathology report showed positive indicators in her lymph nodes and cancer in the lining of her body.

Janet was uncomfortable with the tube down her throat, and I was uncomfortable with the hospital placing unsavory individuals in the room as roommates. I began to make trouble for the staff, demanding a private room for Janet. The roommates kept Janet awake. Some were making phone calls for street drugs. One was phoning a child who lived out of state at all hours of the night. I hated it and lost my patience with the hospital. One evening, while Janet slept and I dozed off in the chair, I witnessed a worker looking through her pocketbook. I'd had enough. I called for a nurse and screamed that we were to be moved to a private room and that no dirt balls were allowed near us. I became an elitist.

When the tube was removed, Janet felt better, and she became talkative. She was optimistic, and after another week, she felt good enough to return home. She missed her dog, Pookie, and she missed working on the racetrack saddle towels, the cloths that indicate the horse's name and number.

We also needed to make an appointment for a port to be placed in her chest and chemotherapy to begin. But first Janet had to completely recover from the surgery. Then we would visit Joe Kaplan for a discussion on chemotherapy, a word that neither of us had thought we would have to entertain at this moment of our lives.

I needed selfishly for Janet Turcotte to survive. She was so close to me that she felt like an appendage. I had shared the best laughter of my life with her. For years, since she loved monogramming the saddle towels for the Maryland races as well as for the Preakness Stakes, I'd watched her slave away and create beautiful saddle towels. She did this to pad her income as a dental hygienist.

Previous to her surgery, one day, Janet phoned me and said simply, "Tracey, I messed up."

I asked, "How?"

She said, "I received the order from the racetrack with a list of horses' names to print onto the saddle towels and saw the name 'Gentlemen.' I thought it was an obvious error on the track's part, so I corrected it to 'Gentleman.'"

On May 10, 1997, a horse had won the prestigious Pimlico Special with Hall of Fame jockey Gary Stevens in the saddle. As the horse had crossed the finish line, a ton of pictures had been taken. The track had immediately noticed the misspelling. The horse named Gentlemen, in the camera's eye, had instantly become Gentleman. No one was happy with Janet. She was quite concerned.

I said, "Well, Janet, I think your reasoning was correct. Who on earth would name a singular horse a plural name?"

We always had each other's backs. Neither of us could do any wrong in each other's eyes. We cheered each other's accomplishments and comforted each other when life threw a couple of foul balls our way. I wanted more memories with her and now this cancer thing was in the way.

When it was time to visit Joe Kaplan at his office in Olney, Maryland, Janet and I were upbeat. We had done our research on colon cancer and conversed with many who'd had the disease. As we drove, we wondered how many hours she would have to endure during each session of chemotherapy. We estimated about four hours, which seemed pretty horrific for her little body.

We sat on one side of Joe's desk, waiting for his entrance. Joe came in, sat down, and immediately got serious. He reviewed the pathology findings and then took out a little chart. We asked him how many hours Janet would have to be hooked up to chemotherapy, and he said, "Let me see ... let me look here ... Let me see what kind of recipe will kill this thing ..." Then he looked up at both of us and said, "Janet will do fifty-six hours of chemotherapy every two weeks."

Fifty-six hours! Janet and I looked at each other, and for the life of me, we do not know why, we started to laugh. We kept laughing and laughing and saying funny things like, "Expect the hair to be gone on the first day," and, "Wow, Janet will be able to light up Central Park." We were laughing so hard that Joe excused himself, got up, and left the room for a bit. He came back to us only to schedule an appointment for the installation of Janet's port and bid us adieu.

As we left Joe's office, a secretary handed us a straw basket with small gray stones emblazoned with the words *Hope, Faith, Survival,* and *Love* and told us to take one. Again we started to laugh. We determined that if we took one, we would be part of the dying, and we surely were not going to think about that. We had more fun to conquer after we'd pushed a few cancer cells out of Janet's body. Then we started to cry. We cried all the way home.

After Janet had her port placed in her chest, she successfully completed fifty-six hours of chemotherapy for fifteen sessions every two weeks. Unfortunately, along the way, the cancer spread to her spleen and belly button, and she had to have both excised. I was there for each of her sessions, and to say that she went to death's door and came out fighting was to say the least. She had to give up her job as a dental hygienist due to the neuropathy in her fingers, but she still managed to create saddle towels for the racetrack. She was healthy enough to maintain a bit of a social life with me, doing her best to project a stiff upper lip.

After a grueling year of hospitals and medical sessions, we decided to take our usual trip to Saratoga to enjoy the August racing meet. She wanted to see Ron Turcotte, her brother-in-law, and the best way to see him was to attend the Hall of Fame inductions.

Upon our arrival in Saratoga, she urged me to do a few things that were routine to her. Our route upon arrival was always the same. I would drive her down Broadway to show her the shops and restaurants, we'd continue driving down Broadway to the lovely summer homes that lined the street and past the Skidmore College campus, and then we'd head off to Union Avenue past the Racing Museum and racetrack and over the bridge to the Saratoga Lake. For some unknown reason, she always liked to drive past former jockey Jerry Bailey's house. I urged her to remove this part of the tour, but she liked seeing the backyard abutting the lake. We would register, year after year at the Longfellows Hotel to the very warm welcome of Dan Fortier, the hotel manager. Danny was aware that Janet was suffering with colon cancer, and he accommodated us with a suite with two bathrooms.

Janet was energized and wanted to go to the track, so we headed off in our flowered dresses to catch a few races. She mentioned visiting her friend, the racing secretary, to attempt to get more saddlecloth business. While in the racing secretary's office, we sat on a couch with a dark-haired man with his head in the *Racing Form*. Janet leaned over to me and said, "That is the horse trainer named Bobby Frankel. I can't stand him because he dates young girls."

I leaned back over to Janet and informed her that either my sister

Tricia or my dear girlfriend Josephine had dated Bobby, but I could not remember which.

That evening, we ate dinner at the premier spot, Siros. It was a fun restaurant and a perfect hangout for trainers, owners, and fans to sit back and relax and digest the food, along with their wins and losses for the day. My daughter joined us, and we were decked out from head to toe. As we were being walked to our table, I felt a tap on my shoulder and turned around.

It was Bobby Frankel. He said, "Are you Tricia, Buddy J's daughter? A friend of mine just said, 'There goes Tricia, Bobby J's daughter.'"

As we got older, Tricia and I looked like twins, and people always got us confused. Bobby Frankel was definitely confused.

"Which friend?" I asked.

He pointed to Tony Dutrow, who was sitting at a table with Bobby's young daughter, Bethenny. I had grown up with Tony. I looked at Bobby and said with a laugh, "Well, Tony should know better than that. I am the pretty sister, Tracey."

He laughed and guided us to Tony.

I turned to Janet and said, "Mystery solved. Tricia dated Bobby Frankel."

IN 2006, THE CROWD FAVORITE horse, Barbaro, won the Kentucky Derby. Going into the Kentucky Derby, Barbaro was undefeated. Barbaro won the Kentucky Derby by the largest margin of victory for any Kentucky Derby since 1946. Maryland fans also cheered Barbaro because jockey Edgar Prado, Barbaro's rider, had ridden in Maryland for many years. The fans loved Edgar. Janet was so excited to be printing the name Barbaro on the Preakness saddlecloth that she brought the towel over to my house so that I could take a picture.

She was also given permission to place the colon cancer logo conspicuously on each of the Preakness cloths, so news stations were calling and interviewing her. CNN did a great segment on the Preakness that included an interview with Janet, and she mentioned the logo and the fact that she had colon cancer. Seeing my dear friend getting a bit of attention felt good. The Preakness week was hers.

Janet, as was customary, attended the Alibi breakfast, a time when all the owners and trainers get together at the Pimlico clubhouse to eat and just kid around with one another. All of the Preakness saddle towels were on display, and Janet was becoming a mini spokesperson for colon cancer awareness. I teased her and said that her press coverage made her a "prom queen." Jerry Bailey who retired and was now a sports commentator mentioned Janet on national tv.

Like Janet, the country was also getting excited about the possibility of seeing another Triple Crown winner. No horse had won the Triple Crown since Affirmed, ridden by a young Steve Cauthen had done so in 1978.

Those who know me generally understand that no events can occur on Kentucky Derby Day, Preakness Day, or Belmont Day. Somehow, my husband's best friend, Noah, forgot about that little friendly stipulation and decided to hold his wedding in Buffalo, New York on Preakness Day. My son, daughter, husband, and I were in attendance, but I was sneaking away to talk to Janet, who was at the Preakness drinking Black-Eyed Susans, the Preakness drink, and enjoying her "fame." I kept a steady eye on my watch, and as soon as the bride and groom completed their vows, I made a beeline directly to the bar and plopped down in front of a television. I phoned Janet, and it was great to hear that she was having so much fun at the Preakness. Janet mentioned that there were so many people in attendance that she could not really see the race, so I told her I would keep her on the phone with the results.

At the Preakness, the band played the song, "Maryland, My Maryland," and the official post parade with the introduction of the horses began. I always got so nervous when the horses walked onto the track and to the starting gate. For some reason, I was exceptionally nervous that day. While all of the horses were in line, something peculiar happened. Barbaro had a false start and bolted out of the starting gate. He then had to be guided back into gate position. I cannot remember a time when I'd ever witnessed that. I kept Janet informed about what was happening.

With great anticipation, I watched and prayed for Barbaro to win so that racing could have another chance at a Triple Crown. I was also happy for Edgar, a jockey who my father was fond of. My father was enthusiastically watching the race as a racing steward, and he spoke to each rider before the race began, wishing them each good luck and safety. The doors to the gate opened and the fans cheered with delight.

Then a catastrophe occurred. As Barbaro began to pass the grandstand at the beginning of the race, he broke his right hind leg, and his foot was dangling for all the world to see. Edgar jumped off his mount and leaned up against the horse to balance him. I could see the colon cancer logo next to the name Barbaro on his blue saddlecloth as he attempted to regain his balance. The world would soon learn that Barbaro had broken his right hind leg in twenty places; he'd broken a cannon bone, a sesamoid bone, and a long pastern bone. His left fetlock joint was also dislocated. These were life-threatening injuries.

Janet kept saying, "Tracey, tell me what is happening. I can't see anything." I did not want to inform Janet because she always saw some kind of symbolism in things like that. She would interpret the situation as a symbol that she, like Barbaro, was breaking down. The week had been so much fun for her that I did not want to temper the mood. I began to gently repeat to her what was being shown on television.

The horse Bernardini won the race, but there was another issue. While watching Bernardini cross the finish line, one of the television sports anchors said, "Well, you would think the racetrack would get the name of the horse right."

I stared at Bernardini's saddlecloth as he was guided toward the winner's circle. I had Janet on the phone, and I said, "Hey, Janet, Barbaro broke down and another horse won the race, but you spelled the winner's name wrong on the saddlecloth!"

"Who won?" she asked.

"Bernardini," I told her, "but you spelled the name Bernadini."

Janet's prom was about to end. She said, "I am out of here. I am running to my car before they find me."

These were the types of events I would miss. Janet making a blunder. Janet understanding racing and loving racing like I did. Janet being my biggest fan and most trusted confident. Janet making me smile.

Janet was my rock, my confidant, and best friend. She made me laugh when I wanted to cry. My good memories with Janet helped me erase my bad childhood ones. I cherished and respected our friendship.

At one time, another girlfriend asked me the oddest question. She asked me, if God came down to earth and said, "Tracey, I will extinguish all the bad memories of your childhood, but your lifetime memories of Janet will also be extinguished, how would you answer?"

The answer is simple—no deal. That is how important my friendship with Janet was.

CHAPTER TWENTY

———————◆———————

COBBLE HILL AND BEN

AS SUMMER 2006 CAME TO a close, I informed my husband that it was time for us to part ways. I moved to Saratoga Springs, New York, upon learning that our daughter had chosen to attend Skidmore College. It was the happiest I had been since high school with Paul and my time with Dorothy at Allegany College. I embraced Saratoga Springs by attending all the major fund-raising events in the community and making many friends. And since I was not licensed to practice law in New York, I began teaching Substantive Criminal Law and Constitutional Procedure at Hudson Valley Community College. I was happy.

I flew home to be with Janet for her additional chemotherapy and treatment. Her treatment had been transferred to Georgetown University Hospital under the care of Dr. John Marshall.

I was flying back and forth from Saratoga Springs to Washington, DC, to be with Janet. There was so little time to move all of my belongings to New York, so I was staying at the Longfellows Hotel. One evening while in the hotel, a tooth began to throb, and I called the manager, Danny, to see if he could locate a dentist for me. I told Danny that I only needed an examination and a simple x-ray. Danny phoned my hotel room and informed me that Dr. Ben had a 9:00 a.m. opening to see me. I thought that if this Dr. Ben was a good dentist, he would not have an opening the very next morning. Nonetheless, his staff called me and professionally took information regarding my appointment, and I repeated that I only need one x-ray.

The next morning, while sitting in the parking lot of Dr. Ben's office, I made plans with a local friend to eat lunch, and then I called Janet to check on her. Janet was in high spirits and eager to come to Saratoga for a visit and just act like there was no cancer. The moments flew by, and I noticed that I had to get into the dental office so as not to create pandemonium with the dentist's schedule, since he'd been kind enough to see me on such short notice.

I noticed that the dentist's building was quite impressive. I walked into the office, thanked the front receptionist for accommodating me, and began to complete the necessary paperwork. As I was filling out the form, I noticed mothers consoling their children who were patients.

I thought, "Wow, how bad is this guy? These kids are nervous, really nervous."

As I walked down the corridor, I noticed things that looked like couches or beds. I thought how unusual it was to see so many couches along the corridor.

I made a mental note to get one x-ray of tooth number fourteen and then run out of there as quickly as I could.

I also noticed how exceptionally clean the office was. I was placed in a room with one chair and a rather large light blasting on my face. I looked around and noticed no cuspidor, no dental drills, and no x-ray machine. I thought, *What in the world is going on?*

Another young girl in a surgical scrub entered the room wheeling an x-ray machine. I looked at her and said, "Wow, things have changed since my days as a dental hygienist. You can move the x-ray machine now, huh? Do you know how to take an x-ray?"

"Yes," she replied and proceeded to x-ray my tooth.

I asked her if it was double film so that I could take a film home to my dentist.

"No," she said. "But we will give you this film after Dr. Ben looks at you."

Then he came in. I took one look at him and entirely woke up from my mini wine drinking bout of the previous night. He was devastatingly handsome. He came in, stretched out his hand, and said, "Hi." Then he stepped back and leaned against the wall. I took a quick look at him—tall, light skin, lots of hair, and piercing blue eyes. Cute!

He leaned over the view box, looked at the x-ray and said, "There is nothing wrong with your tooth."

I said, "Oh no … It has been throbbing all night and keeping me awake. I broke it and Dr. Starr, who is a periodontist as well as a prosthodontist, put a crown on it."

Dr. Ben turned and gave me a little stare as if to say, *I don't care what another practitioner did. You are in my room right now.*

He turned again, walked back to the wall, and said, "There is nothing wrong with your tooth, but this is what I think you will do. Ms. Cooper, you will go back to Maryland, find an endodontist, and he or she will do a root canal." (I was going to do that!) "The endodontist will frap it up, you will get an infection, and get crappy bone. You will run up here begging for an implant, and I hate to work with crappy bone."

How cocky! But I liked it. I looked at him, leaned to my left, and went to retrieve my purse when he said, "Hold on a minute. Don't leave. What are you doing in Saratoga?"

"Me?" I replied, "Well, I am here to purchase a John Witt condo. Do you know him?"

"John Witt?" he said, "No, I know of him, but I do not know him." Then he said, "You look like a Pallotti High School girl."

I almost jumped out of my skin. How on earth did this man, a complete stranger, know where I'd attended high school?

He then said, "I grew up in Olney, Maryland."

Olney—holy smokes. I had gone to school with a ton of Olney girls, and Joe Kaplan's medical office was located in Olney. I mentioned the girls I'd known from Olney, and he kept saying, "Yes, I know her. Yes, I know her." I also asked him if he knew Joe Kaplan, and he mentioned that Joe had treated his own mother for breast cancer.

"Well, how did you get to Saratoga?" I asked

In a voice dripping with disdain, he replied, "My spouse."

Wow, that did not sound good. I immediately surmised that he was married and probably had small children. I could just sense that he was an older dad.

Then I asked him, "Well, what high school did you graduate from and what year?"

"Sherry High School, class of 1977," he answered.

I was immediately intrigued.

As I was walking down the corridor to leave, I heard him say, "Miss Cooper, if you find me an old friend named Sean Buntson there will be no charge for this appointment." He handed me his card with his e-mail and pointed to his e-mail address.

I said, "Deal! I know where to find Sean."

Then Dr. Ben said, "Sean, like me, attended medical school."

I looked at him and said, "I thought you were a dentist."

He replied, "Well, I attended dental school first and then went on to medical school."

"You must like taking tests. I would stress out every time I went to see my law school results which were posted on the wall. The tests were brutal. I can't even imagine taking tests to graduate from both dental school and medical school," I said and proceeded to walk out the door.

———•———

THAT IS HOW I MET Ben, and that was when our relationship began. It was fast and furious and charged by high-powered sparks. I had fled my lonely marriage and made way for a new life.

I loved Ben with just as much love as I had directed toward Paul Wayne so long ago. Ben even informed me that he played in a band called Wayne Drive, so I thought that was pretty cool.

Unfortunately, my union with Ben created complete pandemonium. He was very unhappy in his marriage but had not quite communicated that to his wife when we started our love affair. Shocked when he approached her for a divorce, she became angry and hired an attorney using her best arsenal to torture both him and me.

Ben and his wife had two young boys who were caught in the crosshairs, and their mom and dad learned to hate one another and made sure the boys knew that.

On my end, there was also pandemonium. My spouse was not happy that his intact life was imploding. But after he took thirty-six weeks of vacation within a three-year period without me, I sought better emotional ground and told my husband I had fallen in love with Ben and that I was going to be with him.

Moving to New York was a happy moment but a tiring act. Ben's divorce was heated almost daily, and my divorce reaped some drama of its own. Determined, I moved forward, taking one day at a time. Eventually, things started to settle down, and I could see not only the beautiful Adirondack Mountains but the beauty of my daughter flourishing and a new hope for a great life

Initially, I rented a great condo built by John Witt while waiting for another condo to be built. That development never came to fruition, so I reached out to John and contracted with him to purchase one of the other condos he was building. The market stumbled, and that particular building was never built either, so I went looking for a single-family home and located one on Cobble Hill Drive in Wilton, just outside Saratoga.

I was driving on Cobble Hill Drive and saw some construction in an area of already built homes. One home was under roof, so I decided to take a peek. While I was walking around, a man entered and asked, "Who are you? And what are you doing in here?"

I introduced myself and said, "I think I would like to buy this home."

He replied, "Well, you will have to see the builder about that. That builder is me, and I am not selling it. I am using this place for the Showcase of Homes tour."

I pushed. "Well, I am already approved for my loan and ready to rock."

He and I walked out onto the driveway. He turned to me and said, "Okay. I will sell it to you. What do you do for a living?"

"I am an attorney and a professor," I told him.

He turned and said, "Ugh."

I moved into my beautiful new home in March 2008.

My daughter and I loved the home. I made it an oasis for us. It was not like the home I had grown up in. It was not a house of terror. It was lively. It was pretty. It smelled like flowers and not Clorox bleach. There were no screams or arguments. It was all positive, and I worked hard to maintain that theme, especially since my daughter was feeling the effects of my divorce from her dad. I made our new home as comfortable as I possibly could.

Ben and I had fun selecting many of the options that had not already been ordered through the builder. We were very much in love, and everyone who came across us could see it. Ben was striking. Tall and he thin, he had lots of hair and piercing blue eyes. Upon meeting him in Saratoga, he told me that he had grown up not far from me, so right away, I felt a safe connection. He also told me that he'd played music at a racetrack dive called the California Inn and noted that, during those days, he had been a bit lost and unfocused. Once he did get focused, he'd followed a track of education that few could endure.

Ben told me that, realizing that living around the Beltway required a good income, he'd enrolled in dental school, studied hard and graduated top of his class. Then he took his dental degree and used it to pave his way into advanced standing for medical school and earned a medical degree. So my nickname for him was "Doctor Doctor" because he was both a dentist and a physician. To say that I'd met my ambitious match was to say the least. He could intellectually go toe to toe with me. And because he'd achieved so much on his own, I had huge respect for him and put him on a pedestal that no one except seventeen-year-old Paul had sat on.

As a Saratoga plastic surgeon and oral maxillary facial surgeon, Ben did well. He had two cute boys, and he too deserved a bit of love and attention. Ben was a good guy, and he appeared to adore me. I took that adoration and soaked it up like a sponge. He was handsome, and we complemented one another. I also loved the feeling that I had a protector, and I adopted the expression that we watched each other's backs to describe our dynamics. We became a presence around Saratoga.

Although I did not like my record of two failed marriages, I would have married Ben in a heartbeat. We laughed. We did things together that we both enjoyed. Although his temper flared occasionally, I concluded that it was just steam from a long and tedious day.

Initially, my daughter was quite distant, but over time, she learned to love Ben and share her world with him. My daughter was getting accustomed to his presence in the house, and together with her little dog, Bonsai, we became a cohesive family.

WHILE I WAS ENJOYING MY teaching job and new life, Janet was saying good-bye to hers. She began to decline. The cancer was now in her liver. Thinking that she could have the tumor thermally ablated, she ended up with a large portion excised, and she barely recovered. She was in clinical trials that were taking a toll on her. Her PET scans proved that the cancer was winning, so she decided to get one last consult at the University of Maryland. The physician informed Janet that she had approximately seven days to live.

So Janet went home to die. On the seventh day, as I was preparing to fly to Maryland, Janet's daughter Stacey called, informing me that Janet had passed away in the early hours of the morning. Since that day, I have felt a void like no other and a loneliness reserved just for me.

Somehow I managed to continue teaching my students at the college in Troy, New York. Without those students and their sweet dispositions, I think I would have thrown myself off a cliff. They took my mind off of the four-year journey with Janet, Ben's divorce, my divorce, and my own health issues. Like the reprieve I felt with Paul, Dorothy and Kitty, I felt a reprieve every time I walked into a classroom to lecture.

Janet's funeral was agonizing. I was prepared for her demise, but I wasn't prepared to live a life without my life raft. Janet was my life raft. She cheered me on and put my past in perspective. She made me count my blessings rather than seeing the glass half empty. Now I was to walk alone and to learn to remind myself what she taught me. She taught me to let go.

After recovering from Janet's death, it was time to prepare for fall and for the holidays and to just sit back and thank God that I had such a wonderful friend and confidant in Janet for all those years.

CHAPTER TWENTY-ONE

THANKSGIVING VISITOR

IT WAS 2008, AND BEN and I felt rock solid. We were excited about the holidays. We were settling into the house and loving our time together. We basically worked hard during the day, came home, and closed the door, leaving the world outside. It was great. We planned too preparing a Thanksgiving meal alone.

Then one day the phone rang. The woman I called our mother was calling "to discuss plans for Thanksgiving." I had not seen her in quite some time, but just the sound of the suggestion that we celebrate together made me a bit hesitant. Things always went poorly when she came over and joined what typically was a joyous event. But my father had passed away and although she was dating an elderly man, the relationship was new and I was not sure if they would spend Thanksgiving together.

I tossed and turned at bedtime, trying to decide what to do. I kept hearing Janet's voice: *Just let go. She is your mother. Just ignore the bad and take in the good.*

But what good?

Again, the dutiful side of me came through. I was on the phone with our mother again, and she was complaining that she had seven children and nowhere to celebrate Thanksgiving. Then the words just blurted out or me: "Do you want to come here to Saratoga?"

She immediately responded in the affirmative.

Now in five days, she would arrive for a four-day stay. She insisted on going to Saratoga National, a great golf course with a spectacular Thanksgiving meal for our Thanksgiving dinner.

When Ben came home, I informed him that our mother was coming for Thanksgiving. He asked me how I felt about that. We sat and discussed the merits of her arrival. Always optimistic, I yearned for normalcy with her. I expected that she would be mellow, knowing that I was the one child out of seven who put out the welcome mat.

I got busy with the chore of organizing great food to eat. I chose foods she loved. I made homemade potato salad with bacon, cold Italian string beans, cream cheese Jell-O mold, sausage and rice, and spinach torte. I bought salad greens and baked the infamous family pound cake and some brownies. Our mother loved my pork roast and orange ginger sauce, so that would surely make her happy. I think I did this to gain some sort of approval from her—to do it right. I was attempting to not get "punished" for doing the wrong thing by making the wrong food. My people pleaser coping mechanism was coming out in the form of cooking. While I was growing up, our mother had been critical of any cooking I'd tried to do, any place setting I'd created, any dish I'd washed. I didn't think I could take criticism at this juncture, and I began to feel nervous.

Because our mother did not utilize a cell phone, I contacted her the night before her journey to plan her arrival time. She reassured me that she would phone me once she was ready to leave, and then I'd have a good idea of her arrival time. Typically, the drive from Baltimore to Saratoga Springs would take seven hours, and the New

Jersey Turnpike construction was in high gear. I surmised that she would probably stop twice to grab some food, use the bathroom, and stretch her legs. I was acutely aware that she was a fast driver.

So, I woke up early on the day of her arrival, placed fresh sheets on her bed. She would have the entire second floor to herself. I dusted and scrubbed the unused bathroom and placed flowers in the bedroom and bath. I cleared a great spot in the closet and emptied some drawers in case she wanted some drawer space. I pulled out the Crock-Pot and prepared her favorite pork loin with orange ginger sauce. At the island counter, I placed beautiful place mats and china. She would probably want to sit down and have a warm meal after her long drive. I presumed that she would be tired and hungry.

I felt really good. I was in love with Ben and loved my new house with the beautiful options that the builder had created. The kitchen was magnificent, the tile placed beautifully, and the deck and patios rocked. I loved my backyard and the little chipmunk that sat at my backdoor waiting for me to place seeds in its path. I glanced out my back door and walked onto my deck and just thanked God for everything I had. My two children were thriving, and I was looking forward to my future in my newfound community. It was a time to give great thanks. As I leaned over my deck balcony, peering out into my wooded backyard, I felt very forgiving and felt like I needed to cleanse myself from the bad memories of my childhood. I was simply looking forward to relaxing with our mother. Surely there would be no hitting. Surely she was easing into old age and had a new perspective on her children. Surely she would find my home beautiful and warm.

My manicurist called and said she was running a bit late, so prior to running out the door for my appointment, I created a pretty note for our mother and taped it to my front door: "Welcome! Thanksgiving here we come! If I am not here, I am only moments away. Come in and relax and smell the good food in the Crock-Pot. The door is open, and the alarm is off. Start eating if you are starving. I am right around the corner and will see you in a few minutes. Love, Tracey."

As I was finishing up my manicure, I was calculating our mother's drive time. She'd left at 6:30 a.m., so I computed that she would be in Saratoga (with Thanksgiving traffic) no earlier than between 12:30 and 1:00 p.m. As my manicurist was completing my nails, I phoned Ben to verify the dinner arrangements at Saratoga National. He commented that the meal would be lovely but expensive. He also mentioned that he would treat us, that I was not to pick up the bill.

When I drove up my driveway, I had to hesitate and laugh for a second. There was her car with its Maryland license tag sitting in front of the garage. She had made it to Saratoga in a record-breaking six hours. Sometimes the drive took me as much as nine or ten hours. She never seemed to get a ticket. I would surmise that, when a highway patrolmen witnessed a little, old, gray-haired lady fly by, he or she just had to let her be.

For some reason, I was anxious and happy to see our mother. The weather was perfect. The new community looked lovely, and I could not wait to show her my new, beautiful home. I decided not to go through the garage but to walk in the front door. As I pushed the door open, I called out, *I Love Lucy* style, "Honey, I'm home! Where is my mother and how on earth did you get here so fast?" I added.

Then I saw what I had not seen in years. Our mother came flying around the corner with clenched teeth and a red face. She lunged at me and hit me and raised her arms up into the air to strike me again.

Shocked, I quickly grabbed both of her arms, avoiding another strike and said, "What is wrong with you? What is wrong? What are you doing? Why are you lunging at me?" I demanded to know what on earth had provoked her to become a firestorm of madness. She was so red and angry.

She took her left foot and slammed it on my foot as I held her arms and she shouted, "You son of a bitch. How dare you not be here to greet me? You fucking son of a bitch."

"Mother, my manicurist was late," I said. "And you got here in record time. Did you not stop? Did you not go to the bathroom during your drive? You have no cell phone so that I can know exactly when you'll arrive."

"Fuck you. I called you this morning," she snapped. "You should have been sitting here waiting for your mother."

As a child, I would cringe when she said awful things—when she would say we were going to eat "shit on toast," or when she referred to my brother as "your fucking brother Buddy," or when she launched insulting verbal assaults against my father. I never got used to it. I never liked it, and I swore I would never say those types of things to my loved ones, or anyone else for that matter. Even today, when I hear the word *fuck* or *fucking*, I think of our mother's language and I cringe.

I wanted to erase her from my presence and take away the evil. Quickly, I had to think of what to do with her. My mind was instructing me to tell her to get her sorry, pathetic ass back in her car and drive back to Maryland, but I could not do that. I took her arm and walked her into my family room, so beautiful with its angled ceiling and skylights. Shaking for even having the nerve to grab ahold of her, I sat her down on my couch and tried to calm her down. I found the strength to straighten her out. I demanded that she recognize my efforts. I asked her if she noticed the pork loin in the Crock-Pot. I asked her if she had seen her bedroom with the smell of sweet flowers. I asked her if she had made a cup of tea, since I'd left a china teacup out on the counter for her and water on the stove.

She was so angry. "I feel like going home because you did not have the decency to open the front door and greet your *motha*," she screamed in her heavy New England accent. "You should have been here to greet me."

How pathetic—this was the "crime" she felt deserved another

episode of horrific, unwarranted rage against me. My crime was not being there when she arrived. How unreasonable and unyielding. My crime when I was just six years old had been using Ajax on her kitchen counter. How on earth had I gotten this pathetic creature as my mother? A lifelong bond with her was my punishment for merely existing. If I grew to be a sap who wanted love and warmth, I sure had lost the lottery where she was concerned.

I think of the many childless women in the world who long to give birth and to hold a daughter in their arms, and the way life deals out the cards seems harsh and cruel. Our unsavory mother had seven children when some women cannot even give birth to one. I guess this is the world's way of balancing the wanted children and the resented children. And the awful thing is that our mother does not care what kind of anger she places in our memory banks. This was another horrible event. She has no remorse, offers no apologies, and performs no acts of contrition. This episode would join the memories of our mother in my mind—yet another instance of unreasonableness and frustration.

I was geared to win this round and to take the high road. I cringed as I spoke to her, but I found the dignity to say, "Please stay. You have nowhere to go for Thanksgiving. Ben has made arrangements for us to eat at the golf course. He is looking forward to seeing you." I lied.

I took the high road. I was not overjoyed with my decision to have her as a guest, but I wanted normalcy and could now see I was not getting it. While speaking to her gently yet sternly, I was determined to not allow her to ruin an event this time. She'd ruined Tricia's relationship with her first boyfriend. She'd ruined Baby's last year in high school by locking her in her room. She'd ruined Anna's toddler years by pulling her hair and creating a silent world for her. She had ruined my awards ceremony, and she'd taken away the opportunity for me to pass mementos on to my own daughter. I was not about to allow her to ruin Thanksgiving.

I settled her down and got to the root of her anger, which was not really my having not been home when she'd arrived. She was dating an elderly man named John, and I started to see that this anger had nothing to do with me. Rather, it stemmed from a detachment from him. I asked her why she had not brought her friend with her and reiterated that he was welcome. She mentioned that John had plans with his family and that he was committed to them. She also admitted that she felt strange without him.

I then did what grandmother Rita had done for me so many years ago, when she'd pulled her car over and put quarters in a payphone so I could call my boyfriend Paul Wayne. I said, "Would you like to go into my office and quietly call John at his sister's house?"

She said yes, so I let her into my office and handed her the phone.

She said, "Tracey Mary, I do not know his sister's number."

I told her we could look it up online. She knew his sister's address, so I plugged that into a search engine, along with her name, and we saw a phone number with a Laurel, Maryland, extension. Johns' sister resided in the same neighborhood as my childhood friends and Paul, in Maryland City.

I dialed the number and handed the phone to her. John answered. She smiled and looked happy then I walked out of the room and closed the door to give her privacy.

While she was on the phone, I broke down a bit, started to cry, and called Ben. Ben was on his way over, and I had to forewarn him of the event that had just occurred. I explained to him that she was out of control, telling him that she had hit me and stepped on my foot.

"I know she is your mother, but you tell her, Tracey, to just get back in the car and drive back to Maryland," Ben said. "Jesus Christ, you have been preparing for her arrival for days. You don't need this shit, Tracey. And quite frankly, neither do I. Think about getting her out of the house."

I thought about his advice, but I could not bring myself to put an elderly woman back in her car after she'd driven six hours to our home. It seemed too cruel. I was too compassionate to think about doing that, even though I had huge disdain for her at that moment.

When our mother completed the call, she came out of the office and was like a different person. John must have calmed her down. I looked at her and asked her if she wanted to sit at the counter and eat the pork loin. Then I started a normal conversation with her. I think I was still slightly shaken from the occurrence, but I persevered. I asked her if she'd hit traffic, and I asked her if she was excited about the golf course dinner. I asked her if she wanted to do anything specific while she was in Saratoga. I took the high road, a very high road. I was determined to make her apologize.

She never apologized. She never ever apologized for her outrageous conduct throughout my life. She never apologized to any of us in any fashion. We found it odd. Apologies go so far in healing wounds or hurt feelings. While she was standing in my home, I thought about how I would want an apology from her before I died. But I knew and still know that an apology will never be forthcoming. She is too smug for that. To apologize would be to admit that she was wrong, and she would never admit a wrongdoing. I just got comfortable realizing that I was expecting too much. I just got very comfortable knowing that she would remain an unhappy human, while I eventually created peace, pleasure, and fulfillment by breaking the cycle of abuse and capturing the best of what life had to offer.

Nonetheless, apology or no apology, she had created a rule that would now apply to my benefit. She was now in *my* house with *my* rules, and I could demand that she leave or insist that she stay. It gave me a small sense of power to know that she was the guest, and I was the master. I felt vindicated on a funny level.

Ben walked in through the garage door. He greeted me with a kiss and a hug and some beautiful flowers from my favorite flower shop, Posey Peddler, and then said hello to our mother. She told him that she was angry that I had not been home waiting for her. She told him that she was very, very angry. Ben was poised and patient and looked at me but told our mother how much I'd done in anticipation of her arrival. He asked her if she liked the house. He asked her if she liked the food I'd prepared. She turned her back and said that the house looked beautiful. Then she said she wanted a piece of pizza. Pizza? How unusual. She was normally a huge homemade food eater, and now she wanted pizza? If I hadn't made food for her and had simply presented her a pizza in a box, boy would I have gotten heat. Now she wanted pizza? To make her happy, Ben said, "Let's go to Caputos, the best pizza shop in Saratoga."

We left the pork loin on the counter, and I just shook my head in disbelief as we loaded into his SUV. Our mother sat in the backseat of the car while Ben drove. Ben and I gave each other alternating sympathetic glances. As our mother jumped out of the backseat to enter the pizza shop, Ben took my hand, leaned over, and said, "The days will fly by. Don't let her get under your skin. The days will go by quickly, and then you can send her sorry, pathetic ass back to Maryland, Tracey. Enough of her. Don't let her ruin things for you."

While in the pizza shop, I still felt like an apology was due me. As I watched this woman who routinely beat and abuse her children eat her pizza, I was hoping she would choke on it. With my luck, Ben would remember his Hippocratic Oath and start resuscitating her. I reflected on the day she'd bolted into the green bathroom—the first time she'd beaten me within an inch of my life. I thought how pathetic she was. After all these years, after years of raising children who had somehow ended up with professional degrees, she still carried an unbelievable amount of anger within her aging body. She was still the same skinny woman with a short haircut and smell of Clorox bleach, only older. *How on earth had I come from her womb?* I asked myself for the umpteenth time. As I was reflecting, Ben was making small talk and urging our mother to talk about her new boyfriend. She smiled only when she spoke of him. I really did not listen. I gave up. I loathed her and decided to do what Ben suggested and just buckle down and let the days go by.

When we got home, our mother watched a bit of television before informing us that she wanted to go to bed. I walked her up the stairs, and she peered into the room. I said, "Everything you need is here. Fresh towels are in the bathroom, and there's lots of space in the other rooms. Make yourself at home. I will not put the alarm on, and I will place some water in the teapot for your cup of tea if you should awaken before me."

She turned as I was walking down the stairs and asked me, "What is your Goddamn daughter doing for Thanksgiving?"

Taken aback but not willing to engage or respond to the negative aspect of that question, I gently turned to her and said, "My daughter is with her dad, but she sent flowers in celebration of Thanksgiving and said to say hello." My daughter had never said hello. She ran in a different direction every time she was near our mother. My daughter felt the devil and wanted no part of her. Our mother was just as cruel to my daughter, who I adored, as she had been to her own children.

Your goddamn daughter—it reminded me of how she'd referred to Buddy as *your fucking brother Buddy* when Buddy got hit by the car at the reservoir. It was just impossible for this woman to be kind to her family.

As I walked into my first-floor bedroom and closed the door behind me, Ben entered from the bathroom. He put his arm around me and slid me into bed. We kept a light on and just talked. We commiserated over our upbringings. He discussed how his father had left his mother while he was in high school and how she'd had to quickly obtain her realtor's license and sell homes to keep the family afloat. We both spoke about how chilling our parents could be, and although Ben had not felt the brunt of physical abuse, he had felt the brunt of abandonment. We both recognized that our children were in a much better place, that they were light in spirit and gleeful in heart.

Ben reviewed his familial history with me. He spoke of his grandmother, a prominent *Vogue* model who was married to George "The Hump" McManus. Hump was in charge of the Irish mob and was very good friends with the infamous Arnold Rothstein, whom he murdered after a night of gambling.

Ben's family was unique. A model, a murderer, and a marriage deserter were among the members, but no physical abuse had taken place in his immediate household. We both had wounds but of a different kind. Ben had watched his mother struggle to the point of exhaustion every day. While taking care of three children, she'd worked so often that she'd ignored the lumps in her breasts that had ultimately taken her life. As the oldest child, Ben had the duty of holding his mother until she took her last breath. It was a monumental moment for him and made him weep upon reflection.

Ben's love for his mother was measured by his warmth for her as she took her last breath. For me, I would never hold our mother when she took her last dying breath. I am hoping that I do not hasten her trip to dying rather than holding her lovingly in my arms. I would want to take a pillow and help her along to hell's gate. When Ben spoke so lovingly about his mother, I could not relate at all. I envied his connection to his mother. I never knew what that felt like. The closest I'd come to experiencing the mother-child bond from the perspective of the child was with Kitty Carson or Dorothy Huff. Thank God for them. These two women gave me a glimpse of what most children feel from their parents.

In the morning, I awoke to our mother reading *The Saratogian*, the local newspaper, and sitting beside her was a cup of tea.

"Good morning," I said.

She looked up and said, "This paper is a little slim. There is nothing in it. My God why do you buy it?" She threw it in the wastebasket.

Ignoring the dark cloud ready to swell in my home, I walked over to the little kitchen table where she sat and asked her if she wanted a toasted bagel or an English muffin. She informed me that she did not want to eat anything in anticipation of our Thanksgiving meal. She spent the hours reading and calling her boyfriend and basically staying still. In reflection, I think she knew that I had spoken to Ben about her little temper tantrum so she was trying to be on good footing for the day.

Ben awoke and was more than nice to her. He asked her if she wanted to take a walk or take a drive or whether she was in need of anything at the pharmacy, which remained open on Thanksgiving. He was so good with her. I wanted a bolt of lightning to come through my skylight and knock her out forever.

Our Thanksgiving meal was delicious, and the venue was perfect. One would think that the ambience would be satisfying to her. But, as usual, nothing pleased her. The golf course was decorated with all the festive fall colors, and the meal was cooked to perfection.

As we sat at the table eating our feast, our mother was not entirely happy. She could be heard muttering various complaints: "Goddamn, I feel a draft." "The stupid waiter forgot to bring me cream." "My fucking back hurts from the trip." She just could not be good and behave. The vitriol somehow slithered out like a wet snake upon the grass. I was so embarrassed.

While she made a visit to the lady's room, I looked at Ben and said, "I am ordering a Cutco knife, and that is what I am going to dig into her body when she is cold and dead."

"You can't do that," he said. "It's a crime in most states, and you know it."

I told him that I did not care; the punishment would be short compared to the infinity she would spend with a knife lodged in her side. I told him that if I was discovered, I would try to gain sympathy from the court by portraying myself like those who'd hit Mussolini's dead upside-down body. Later, I researched crimes against dead bodies. And it is not yet a crime in Maryland to desecrate or mishandle a dead body unless you are a mortician. The thought of not getting punished for stabbing her dead body with a knife made me smile.

On Friday morning, we awoke to barking orders. Our mother wanted another piece of pizza. To keep her steady, we obliged her. Back to Caputos we went. After the pizza, we took her down to Broadway in Saratoga, with its charming shops and restaurants, hoping that would improve her mood. She walked slowly due to her age, but her tongue moved rapidly. As she described each one of her children, the discussion was laced with negativity. She would mention an achievement and then lace it with some derogatory remark. I kept her walking, hoping that her comments wouldn't sink in and make an indelible impression in my mind.

While on Broadway, I noticed that a new cupcake bakery had opened called Betty's Cupcakes. Ben and I peered into the cute window with all its decorations and convinced our mother to sit down and eat a cupcake. The newly opened shop was decorated in a Lucy and Ricky motif. The staff had pretty 1950s skirts on, music was playing, and the cupcakes smelled luscious. The atmosphere was very upbeat. Each of us ordered a yummy cupcake, sat down at a brand-new table, and started to eat the treats.

One of the workers approached our mother, knelt down close to her and asked her, with a smile, if she liked her cupcake. Our mother, turned to look at her and, as direct as an arrow, said, "You won't be in business long. This is the driest Goddamn cupcake I have ever eaten."

Mortified, the employee looked over at me, and I just shook my head. I gathered our sharp-tongued mother up, and we scooted out of there as quickly as we could. I never visited Betty's Cupcakes again. I was so ashamed and embarrassed of our mother.

I vowed that I would exhaust her on Broadway so that she would fold into bed like a boulder hitting the ocean floor. After we walked, Ben drove us around for hours just to knock her out. When we got home, she said, "Tracey, I am going upstairs to pack, and I will see you in the morning." Mission accomplished! She was exhausted, and now I did not have to listen to one more negative word coming out of her mouth.

On the morning she was to leave, I woke up whistling. I was so happy to be getting rid of her. I walked into the kitchen and again found her sipping tea.

"Hey, Mom, give me your car keys," I said. "I know you don't like to fill your car up with gasoline yourself. Let me take it to the corner gas station and fill it up for you."

She said, "Thank you, Tracey," and handed me her keys.

Elated, I drove to the gas station and filled her tank to the brim. Noticing dead bugs on her windshield from the drive up to Saratoga, I used the window scrubber to wash her front window and rear window.

I turned up the music and sang all the way back to my house, modifying the lyrics to a well-known tune: "I am going to wash that witch right outta my hair."

The witch was going to be gone in about fifteen minutes. When I drove up my driveway, she was already outside with suitcase in hand and a stern look on her face. Yay! I handed her the keys and said, "This full tank of gas will get you home, so no worries. Be careful and let me know when you arrive home."

She gave me a little hug and then got in the driver's seat. A look of horror came over her face. She rolled her window down, and I peered in to see what the problem was.

She clenched her teeth and said, "You Goddamn idiot. Did you clean my windows?"

"Why yes," I responded. "I did clean your windows because there were so many bugs on them."

"Well, now I have to stop and clean your mess," she snapped. "There are so many streaks on my windows. You will never make a good window washer, Tracey Mary. Just stick with whatever the hell you do and thanks for messing up my windows."

I stood up, waved good-bye, and muttered, "And thanks for being the meanest mother in the neighborhood. Good riddance, and thanks for making Thanksgiving miserable."

I often wondered why I placed myself in harm's way repeatedly. I can only presume it was because this woman was our mother. I felt a certain responsibility to continue some form of mother-daughter relationship. Maybe it was my attempt at creating normalcy. Even though my efforts continuously failed, the hope of having a peaceful connection always existed.

After Thanksgiving, my desire to create a peaceful existence or maintain a type of connection with our mother waned. It no longer bothered me that we didn't have that, and I accepted that a connection or normal relationship with her was an impossibility. As an adult, I realized that it was not my fault that we had not created normalcy; it was her flaws that prevented it. Yet I wondered why I'd chosen not to sever the ties completely. It perplexed me that I continued to place myself in her presence.

I had done my duty. The experience had not been good, and I made a vow to resist her whining about having nowhere to go for the holiday in the future. Her presence was like a dark cloud over a brilliant sunshine. She was such a tormented person that she ended up tormenting everyone around her. I think there comes a time when you just have to let go. There is no positive need to keep such negativity around. There is no rule that a person must continue to grace us with his or her presence just because of a biological relationship.

As a child, I had believed such a rule existed, although I am not sure I could have told you who I thought made the rule up. And back then, I had stood by that rule because it was forced upon us from God knows who. I just no longer believe biology should force us to connect to a lifetime of pain. Be gone, I told that pain. I did not need it in my life anymore. I was not responsible for our mother. I decided I no longer had a moral obligation to her. To obey that moral doctrine meant placing someone who was very immoral in my path. Be gone, I told that "rule." I did not want it.

Tricia did not speak to our mother for twenty years. During that time, she became a physician and remained on the West Coast. For Christmas, I would sign Tricia's name to my parents' gifts so that my father would not feel badly. After all, Tricia's emotional distance was really aimed at our mother and not him. Robby also resided in California, his home since he was eighteen years old. Anna moved to Florida at age nineteen and remains there. And Baby resides in Massachusetts, where she has resided since she graduated from college. Buddy is the hardest worker I have ever seen. He loves working on a farm and is in a good relationship with a nice woman. Mitzy is employed as a waitress and probably has saved more money than any of us. She is the only sibling who never had a child.

Throughout my life, I was a Marylander and, thus, included our parents in the normal happenings of life, like my children's dance and piano recitals, school functions, parties, and large holiday gatherings at my home. My siblings speak to our mother just to get the obligatory weekend conversation over with. But I stuck with the obligations and rituals and included her in events and happenings. I hated it. It was time for another sibling to take over.

To this day, I am not sure why our mother is so miserable. She has beautiful children and amazing grandchildren who are beautiful and accomplished. Janet would always say that the family children and grandchildren were intimidating because everyone was so attractive and successful. Janet knew how our mother was. She knew about the abuse. So when Janet lay at Georgetown University Hospital under the watchful eyes of those who ran the colon cancer unit, she would look up at me with her chemotherapy drip in her arm and say, "The reason your mother has no cancer is because she screams the cancer cells out of her body, and the cancer is too afraid to stay inside of her."

Janet was right. Even cancer was afraid of our mother.

Chapter Twenty-Two

Legos and the Will

BEN'S YOUNGEST SON, RONNIE, LOVED putting Legos together. So it was natural that he wanted a Lego kit for his seventh birthday. So I decided to take him to Toys "R" Us to peruse the Lego section and select a birthday Lego kit. Typically, when I would purchase a Lego kit for Ronnie, it ranged in price from seven to fifteen dollars. On this particular day, while gleaning the shelf with joy, Ronnie pointed to a large Lego kit with an airplane depicted on the box, for $200. I obliged but told him he could not receive it until his birthday. While he was asleep, I began the process of putting the pieces together, an impossible feat. My son had worked at a hobby store years prior and had become a master at putting remote control cars together, so I phoned him and asked if he would oblige. I put the pieces in separate Ziploc bags and shipped the entire package to my son.

My son said completing the project took many painstaking hours. Proud of the construction, he sent me a picture of the plane, and I happily showed it to Ronnie. I promised Ronnie that, when I flew to

Maryland, I would retrieve the gift for him. Within weeks, I was in Maryland and ready to pick the plane up for Ronnie. Upon seeing it, I realized that it would break into pieces in the overhead bin of a flight, so I again called Ronnie and promised that I would drive my car from New York to Maryland to retrieve his gift. My son brought the plane to our mother's house, and I asked her if I could place it in an unused closet in the guest room, where it would be safe and out of sight until I could return to Maryland with my car. As I gently placed the Lego plane on the floor, I noticed that there was nothing in the closet, not even a hanger.

The winter weather in 2008 was brutal, and I was scared to drive my car to Maryland, so I waited for the first clear road to drive back. When I was close to our mother's house, I phoned her to inform her of my anticipated arrival. She said she would put a cup of tea on the stove. Exhausted, I entered her house, and the tea tasted great. Our mother filled me in on many happenings, and I almost forgot why I had come to her house.

I said, "Oh my gosh, I almost forgot to grab the plane."

She looked at me and said, "The plane? Ronnie's plane? I decided to give that Lego set to the local Episcopal church for their auction."

I looked at her. "What?" I asked. "Why on earth would you do that? That was Ronnie's gift. He is expecting it. You had no right to arbitrarily give that present away. Are you joking me or pulling my leg? You knew I was driving hours to come retrieve it for the boy."

She replied, "Ronnie does not need it, and it was taking up space in the closet. I was tired of looking at it."

"Mother, there was nothing in the closet, and no one went in that closet to get bothered by it," I said.

"Well, I did," she retorted.

I stood up. "Well, guess what? I did not drive down here for nothing, and my son did not spend hours assembling the plane only for it to be given away. So what you are going to do is march down to the church and apologize for the misunderstanding but you need to retrieve the plane and bring it home because it belongs to a little boy from New York. The other alternative is to give me two hundred dollars to buy Ronnie a new one." I told her that I was not happy. I wanted to hit her on top of her head to try to knock some sense into her.

Our mother chose retrieving the plane from the church. She brought it home within hours of it being auctioned off. I remembered how she'd discarded my mementos, trophies, and baby furniture. She'd had no right to discard them, but she had done it because she could curry favor with someone else and look like the do-gooder she wanted people to believe she was. She gave the baby furniture to her friend's daughter to look like a hero. She gave the 350 trophies I'd collected to charity to look like a hero. She'd thrown my mementos away on a whim. She had given the plane away to look like a hero. This time, her plan to convey property that did not belong to her had not worked.

Again, like a million other times, I sat in the chair numb, stunned by her actions. I was really done with dealing with her. I wanted one of my other siblings to take the duty of her from me. What was so innately wrong with this woman?

ASIDE FROM ATTEMPTING TO FIGURE out what made our mother tick, as children my siblings and I could never totally be sure how the residual effects of the trauma weaved their way into our daily decisions. But one thing was certain and irrefutable—between my siblings and I, there were a high number of divorces and ended relationships. As adults, all of our first marriages, with the exception of Baby's first and only marriage, were exit ramp marriages. Although we attempted to make the marriages work, they did not.

As my relationship with Ben continued, I began to see he had anger issues. While in Las Vegas for a getaway trip, he took a phone call from his attorney, hung up the phone, and started throwing things and kicking the furniture and trash can. While we were sitting on the plane that would take us home, prior to takeoff, he picked up the phone, listened again to his attorney, and screamed so loudly that my contact lens popped out of my left eye. On another trip, this one to Canada, his BMW stalled. He slammed his fist against the windshield and screamed so loudly that I thought I should jump out of the car. These outbursts were a habit during our road trips. Something would tick him off, and he would explode. Like our mother's anger, Ben's anger was too extreme for the events that had triggered it. He one day drove over a bridge. I mentioned that I thought he'd missed the correct exit ramp. He realized his simple error and could have easily turned around but instead began to scream and sweat. His response to simple errors seemed unreasonable.

At home, I reached out to a law client of mine who was a therapist and presented the events to him. His advice? Run. He said, "Tracey, with everything you experienced with your mother, you do not need more bad events. Just tell Ben to go away. You need peace."

Yes, I needed peace. So I sat Ben down and told him more about my violent upbringing. I explained how sensitive I was to screaming and yelling. He continued to have temper tantrums. At one point, he lashed out at his two small sons. I picked them up, grabbed my car keys, and literally threw them in my car and drove them away. I was not about to watch as innocent children were abused on any level. I had witnessed enough abuse in my lifetime.

After the incident with the children, Ben calmed down and tried hard to be cognizant of my low tolerance for yelling and screaming. I had been so excited about my new life in New York and excited to challenge myself by taking the New York Bar Exam. I was now fifty years old, but I felt that my ability to concentrate was good.

I enrolled in a few classes at the University of Albany Law School and proceeded to prepare for the dreaded New York exam. I was so happy with my home and my new connections in Saratoga that I felt strong enough for this challenge. As I drove into Albany, I remember pulling off on the side of the road while listening to a beautiful song and hastily jotting the words down, thinking that the words would be fitting of marriage vows. I was elated and fulfilled as a woman. I tried to put Ben's temper episodes out of my brain and balanced the magnitude of our chemistry against the backdrop of outbursts.

On one particular day about seven days prior to the bar exam, I asked Ben if I could use his computer to watch a law lecture, since my daughter was utilizing my computer. He nicely set the computer up for me. With brownie and hot tea in hand, I sat down to watch the information blast on the screen. As I was maneuvering around his keyboard, my law lecture pulled down, and simultaneously, a screen full of online dating sites presented itself. I stared at the sites. Pushing the back button, I could see that Ben had been on the sites a lot because multitudes of sites were evident.

With my heart half-broken, I forced myself to gather my thoughts. I made a fictitious profile and posted an ad on one of the sites. Within one hour, Ben responded to my ad using a fake name. I became pornographic and laced my messages to him with the promise of nothing but future sexual contact with him.

The next day was a Tuesday, a typical day for me to pick up Ben's children at daycare even though he worked only a half day. He messaged me on the dating site and asked to meet me at Starbucks for a hookup. I was aghast, and I was scared. If the person who was e-mailing me was actually Ben, I knew that my life with him would take an unpredicted, sudden turn. I was more than fearful. I prayed that this was not going to happen. I could not fathom thinking about a life without Ben.

With the agreed upon time for our encounter set, I ran out my door, drove to the Starbucks, and parked far enough away that Ben would not see my car. I felt somewhat ridiculous. After all, if my efforts proved me wrong, I was wasting a ton of time when I should have been focused on studying for the bar exam. I sat quietly in a far spot in the Starbucks, watching the glass door for customers coming and going.

Just as I was ready to leave, I looked up, and I saw Ben enter. He looked amazing. His hair was shiny. His skin was glowing. He was pumped. He was ready. I turned toward him as he walked close to my chair, and he said, "What the hell are you doing here? I thought you were studying."

I responded, "The better question is what are *you* doing here?"

He said, "I have no idea what you mean by that."

I stood up and looked him in the eye. "I am the one you have been e-mailing on the dating site," I told him.

"What kind of games are you playing?" he demanded.

"Me?" I asked. "What kind of games are *you* playing? I should be picking your children up at daycare, and while I am taking care of your boys, you are out here doing this."

Ben ran out of the Starbucks. I followed behind.

"Ben, we need to talk about this. We need to talk about this," I begged.

He yelled back while literally running to his car, "I will see you later at home. I will get the kids."

So, that was the beginning of the end of my grand love affair in New York. I felt like a fish gasping for air on the sidewalk. I got back into my car and I could not breathe.

I immediately went to my gynecologist and got examined. Thankfully, I had no sexually transmitted diseases. I also failed the New York bar exam because I could not concentrate.

I struggled. I cried. I got sad. I went to bed. I could not breathe. My daughter begged me to get out of bed. It was difficult. I loved him. I could not reason why this had happened. Like I'd kept my memento box under my childhood bed, I kept an antique hamper with all of Ben's cards, letters, notes, and messages. The hamper was filled with things. Ben was so romantic when it came to flowers and gifts and candy that the hamper was full. I turned the hamper over one afternoon, sat on the floor, and read the romantic cards and letters. With such words of intimacy and love, what did I not see that created a void in him—that made him need to reach out to the web of strangers on the Internet? We had sex two, three times a day, every day. We were connected. We laughed, and we had fun. We were completely satisfied emotionally, physically, and intellectually.

I kept thinking about how, years prior to this event, Paul had sat me down and told me that he'd gotten another girl pregnant. That was the first time, aside from our mother's strikes, that I'd felt a blow to my stomach. Now it was happening all over again.

So, for the first time in my life, I sought psychiatric counseling. The issue with Ben was too big for me to handle. I had to make some finite decisions on an emotional as well as a financial level. I was very concerned about my finances. I had invested in a home. The market was bleak, and if I sold it, I would surely lose money. I loved New York, but I knew that if I stayed, I would continue taking care of Ben's boys—that I would remain in the relationship as if none of what I'd discovered had happened. I began to resent the energy I spent on the children. I began to resent taking care of his home and grocery shopping for them and cleaning up after them.

Ben dragged me to his therapist in hopes of mending things, but first I sent his therapist the links of messages on the dating site so he could get a flavor of what had transpired. Ben informed me that he'd prefaced the meeting with some discussion with the therapist about my upbringing. So as I walked into the therapist's office, I knew that he was aware of the baggage I carried in my brain.

The therapist was a nice man, self-assured but humble. His office was messy and poorly decorated. It was outdated, plain, and stark. He sat in a simple chair, and Ben and I sat in chairs across from him. I began the conversation. I spoke to the therapist. "I know you cannot mend things with one session, but to get the most out of this hour, I want you to know that I come to you with childhood wounds. I came from a family of seven children. Our mother was not a mentally stable woman. She beat us continuously. My father was a gentle soul, but he was ill equipped to break up the family and remove us. But that is not the reason I am here. The reason I am here is because an event with Ben has paralyzed me. I am in an ambiguous spot, and I desperately need some guidance."

The therapist looked me straight in the eyes and asked me to repeat the startling event. After I gave him the details of my encounter with Ben at Starbucks, Ben piped up and said, "Make Tracey love me the way she did. Help her to put me back on the pedestal."

There was complete silence in the room. The therapist looked directly at Ben and said, "I hate to tell you, but Tracey will never be the same."

Ben kept repeating that my issues were deeper than the experience at Starbucks. The therapist kept repeating that what had happened, as an isolated incident, was pretty alarming to a relationship. Ben was begging the therapist to repair the damage. I could see that Ben was desperate and I could also see he was remorseful and was in love with me. But I felt petrified and the deception hurt me. I also felt immense sadness for us. We tried so hard to have that perfect union. But the Starbucks event was irretrievable. It was the elephant in the room. It was not going away.

"Ben informed me that there was a good bit of violence in your home while you were growing up," the therapist said.

"Yes, there was," I agreed. "And due to all the screaming and hitting during my childhood, I have very little tolerance for it today. When Ben gets angry, I recoil. I am on overload. I cannot be in a room with any of it. I insist on zero yelling, screaming, or hitting. During my long marriage, my husband and I screamed at the top of our lungs only once, and that was when my son took the car out for a spin when he was only fifteen. We were so angry thinking that the child could have killed some innocent person."

"Tracey's issues have nothing to do with me," said Ben.

The therapist looked at me and asked, "How do you feel about that statement?"

I replied, "I want you to teach me to get strong enough to leave."

———•———

I CONTINUED WITH THERAPY AND got strong enough to leave. It was not easy. I was still in love with Ben. I discovered that Ben kept secrets and lived a different type of life with needs I could not meet. I did not want to play Colombo and wonder where Ben was or who he was with behind my back, especially while I was taking care of his children. If I delved deeper into my childhood with the therapist, it would mean remaining in New York, and I just could not waste any more time in an ambiguous relationship with Ben.

I loved New York but my law department at the community college lost its funding, and my job was terminated. I had resided In New York for six years, but I was encouraged to return to Maryland to assist my friend in his law practice while he worked on a few huge cases. It saddened me to sell my beautiful home. I again put one foot in front of the other in order to persevere.

Upon my return to Maryland, our mother called and invited me to her home for Easter. She stated it would just be me and her; no other siblings would attend. I told her that I would make some of her favorite dishes—potato salad with bacon, the same cream cheese Jell-O mold and Italian string bean dish I'd prepared on the Thanksgiving when she'd come to visit me, and the famous family pound cake.

I had been working nonstop and was happy that Easter had arrived and my phone would cease ringing with frantic client calls. With a car filled with yummy food, I drove to our mother's neighborhood and rang the doorbell.

She greeted me with, "Take your Goddamn shoes off."

Her home was spotless, and evident vacuum cleaner marks lined the carpeting. There was not one dust particle on the wood floors.

After several trips to the car for the food, the two of us sat down and ate. To my surprise, she ate quickly. I said, "Mother, you never eat dinner quickly. Why are you eating so fast?" She had taken the energy to press a lace tablecloth and put out her finest china.

"What in this house would you like to take?" she asked abruptly.

"What do you mean?" I responded.

"I want you to take what you desire before I die," she said.

"Mother, you are alive," I told her. "I refuse to go through your home like a scavenger hunter and take things. I will not do that."

She looked me squarely in the eyes and said, "Well, the reason I want you to take something is because I did my will."

"Don't tell me about your will, Mother. You do not have to mention anything about that. Please, eat more food. Eat dessert. And then—"

Before I could complete my sentence, she added, "Because I am leaving Mitzy my entire estate. She is the only child who is nice to me."

I was aghast. Mitzy? "What did you say?" I asked her. "Did you say Mitzy is the only child mentioned in your will? Did you say Mitzy is the only child who has been nice to you?"

Then reflecting on my hardworking siblings, I begged, "Mother, what about Robby, who works so hard, and Anna, who slaves at her job every day? And what about Baby and Tricia, who became professionals? They all work so hard. Dad would not like this." I continued, "Mother, I see this happening in my law office all the time. Don't do this. This type of thing tears families apart. You have seven children and a host of grandchildren. Do not do this."

I begged her to reconsider. "How can you say that no one has been nice to you?" I continued. "Please know that I don't want you to favor me in any fashion. What I'm about to say isn't meant to be self-serving because I want nothing. But your statement is so mean to my ears. I included you in every holiday, every party, and every social event. I took you and Dad everywhere. I met doctors with both of you. Don't do this.

"For God's sake, Mitzy sat in the basement while I ran around organizing the going away party when you left the big house. Mitzy sat in the basement for your twenty-fifth wedding anniversary party that I arranged for you. Mitzy sat in the basement for both of our grandfathers' funerals and our grandmother's funeral. She sat in the basement when I organized Dad's surprise seventieth birthday party in the middle of my law school exams. The other siblings have done things from afar too. They have pitched in as best they could from out of state."

I continued, "For God's sake, Mom, Mitzy is not your only child. By including Mitzy as your only child in your will, you are indicating to me that you don't recognize all of your children, only one. This is not the proper thing to do. Dad would not like it. You are smarter than this. There will be resentment toward Mitzy. Don't pull this family in that direction."

She looked me in the eye and said, "I guess you don't want to take anything."

Since dinner was over, I slowly got up, gathered my dishes, and put my shoes on at the front door. I know I was shaking my head in disbelief. I was flabbergasted. I thought about Kitty's' will. Even though one of her children had stayed distant, Kitty had separated her assets into equal divisions among her three children. She'd recognized her grandchildren with gifts and even recognized her son's illegitimate child, one born out of wedlock when her son was very young, as a grandchild. Our mother had always criticized Kitty, but Kitty was a fair human being.

Then I felt a surge of energy charge through me. I placed my dishes on the floor, lightly grabbed her arm, and walked her over to her refrigerator. I was not done with her. "Look at this refrigerator," I said. "What do you see?"

She said, "Pictures of grandchildren."

"Yes," I said, "your grandchildren. So what about them? Do you know how this would hurt their feelings, as if they mean nothing to you? Dad is dead. You are what is left of the older generation. Please reconsider. At least, at a minimum, go to Starbucks, grab some coffee cards, place them in envelopes, and leave each grandchild a little token."

She turned, looked at me, and said, "I could care less about them."

I glared at her. "You know as well as I know that my son is your favorite grandchild," I said. "You are always having him do things for you, like show you how to e-mail. And he lovingly comes over every time you need him. Do not say that he is not special to you."

"I could care less," she said again, her tone dripping with spite.

I asked her if she'd discussed this issue with Mitzy. She said yes, she had discussed her will with Mitzy and Mitzy had no issue with it. Well, our mother had created a monster in Mitzy. Mitzy was still sucking on our mother's breast milk; of course Mitzy thought of herself as the only child.

I thought back on all the dysfunction I had put up with, all the pain I'd endured as I'd tried to carve out a life for myself free of abuse. I had made mistakes—costly, painful ones. I doubted myself. I had relationship problems I was still trying to overcome. Yet, here I was, still trying to make this woman a normal mother. It was suddenly clear to me it was never going to happen, and I needed to be away from her poison before it pulled me back in. At that moment, I realized both she and Mitzy could go to hell. They could keep all of it and the abuse that came with it. Thank God Dad was dead. He would be mortified.

I walked slowly to the door, wanting again to drain her DNA from my body. How on earth could I be related to her? I denied her completely. I loathed every word that came out of her mouth. I still cringed every time she spewed her venom.

I went to the front door and put my shoes on and loaded the dishes into my arms, thinking only of removing myself from this human being's presence. As I opened the door, she said, "I would like you to take me for Greek food on Wednesday."

I looked at her and said, "Mitzy can take you."

I presume our mother spoke to Mitzy and repeated that I was not happy with the instructions in her will. I was told that I was no longer welcome in the house. I truly did not care, but I was in the middle of assisting our mother's boyfriend with some legal issues. I had attended several hearings on his behalf. At the inception of the case, I had flown back and forth from New York a few times to assist him, staying at our mother's house in the guest room to defray the costs. At this time, the case was still pending. I decided that I'd had enough of getting a foot up my rear while I was performing nice deeds.

When I got to the courthouse, I asked to see the judge in chambers and presented him with a withdrawal of appearance. He obliged, so I had one more thing to do.

I asked our mother if I could come over for a cup of tea. We kept the conversation light, but I could not resist bringing up the terms of her will and the slap in the face to the rest of my family. She refused to bend. As I was leaving, she said, "And tell your Goddamn daughter hello." I instantly thought again of how she'd referred to her adorable, blond firstborn son—"your fucking brother Buddy."

Enough is enough, I decided.

At the front door, I drew myself up so I was standing straight and tall, turned to her, and said, "Take a good look at my face, because you are never going to see it again. You are truly a piece of work, and I do not want to be in your company ever again. And by the way, I do not describe my daughter as a 'Goddamn daughter.' I cherish her and thank God every day that she is my daughter. She is such a joy for me. Shame on you." I opened the door, walked out, and slammed the door behind me.

I felt happiness as I drove home. I had done it. I had severed ties. If Kitty were alive, I swear I would be the oldest person to legally denounce a mother and insist that Kitty adopt me as her daughter. I just did not want the label of being that woman's relative for one more second. But the best I could do was to stay away and hope she drifted off in her sleep. I was elated, and I felt light. It was the oddest sensation. I even felt younger. It was as if a glow surrounded me and embraced my soul. I was done.

Chapter Twenty-Three

---◆---

The Pain of Memories

AS MY SIBLINGS AND I married, had children, divorced, and remarried, we acknowledged that our actions in our own homes never mirrored or resembled our mother's actions. We did not abuse our children physically or emotionally. We were and still are extremely kind to our children. We kiss them. We applaud them. We love and adore them. We have guided them to be gracious human beings. My siblings and I discuss the damage we suffered at our mother's hand. We are amazed that we did not continue the cycle of abuse. We conclude that we went to the complete opposite spectrum in raising our children. They were on the receiving end of what we dreamed of. All of our children are amazing individuals. We stand as a testament that you can suffer abuse but turn around and have productive lives and raise warm and loving children.

Even today our mother does not treat us with the respect that we deserve. She is not proud of us or proud of our children. She still directs conversation about us in the negative and not the positive. The greatest freedom for me comes through understanding that, while

I did not have a choice as a child, I have a choice as an adult. And I chose not to have this abuse in my life. I am sad that I had to reject our mother to get the peace I deserve. But I am proud that I have not left the same legacy of abuse to my children, who mean the world to me.

Our mother is still alive. My siblings have very little communication with her. They partake in obligatory phone calls. We constantly abhor how she raised us and how she chose violence over loving kisses. We wait for an apology that will never happen.

Our father, as I mentioned, has passed away. He had terrible twilight years with her. She was cruel to him as he lay dying. At one point, I felt compelled to call social services to report abuse of a vulnerable adult. As I placed my finger on the phone, I just simply could not deal with thinking about her wrath toward me, so I put the phone down. Months later, Tricia, independently mentioned that she too had wanted to call social services.

When my father took his last breath, our mother preferred to sit in the family room rather than join her children in the bedroom to say good-bye to this nice man who had provided her with a good living all her life. She sat stoically in a chair, repeating that she saw no reason to hold his hand.

We wait for her to die. We wonder what words will come to our lips at her funeral. We will show up as if we are closing the door on a brutal lifetime of harm. In my mind, seeing her in a coffin will bring me satisfaction similar to victims watching their perpetrator's execution. I still fantasize about sticking the knife into her side. Then I imagine handing Mitzy the funeral bill, since she was "the only one who was nice" to our mother.

In law school, one of our lectures was about child abuse. The professor was a renowned expert on the topic. I listened intently as he showed us slides and pictures of abuse on a screen. I remember feeling so sorry for the children. I remember thinking that my siblings and I had also been victims of child abuse, yet we had no cigarette burns or belt buckle impressions. We were beat within an inch of our lives almost daily and verbally abused so badly that no amount of soap will wash away the psychological damage we received. Since there was daily abuse, the cumulative effects remain with us.

Often, I surmise that, because we held ourselves out as happy and were attractive, many would doubt the truth. But then people doubted others with well-constructed masks. Consider the pedophilia rampant among Catholic priests. Many disbelieved Marilyn Van Derbur, a former Miss America, when she exposed her father for incest. We are here to say that abuse can happen in any family, no matter how pretty the people are or how hard they work at presenting themselves as happy and accomplished.

We question why our mother never sought help for her anger and resentment, especially since she was educated as a nurse. She could have reached out to a physician or sought out some medication to control her rage. I think our lives would have been much more peaceful. With some guidance from a professional, I think she could have really soared as a good human being. I could see how nicely she treated many people outside our family, so why not get a grip on reality and start treating us nicely too? I do believe that a therapist would have given her some coping skills and strategies for managing seven children. Knowing her as I do, I can surmise that she refrained from seeking medical advice because she did not want to admit her shortcomings. Maybe she was also afraid of being arrested or that we would be taken away.

Oddly, my siblings and I are somewhat respectful of the fact that she is our mother. As I took one last look at her, I stared at her aging face and body and had to remind myself that she had acted the way she had. In her old age, she developed an unusual habit of poking our arms to get our attention. The action felt like a form of hitting to us. It was as if she still needed negative contact. She could not hit us, so she utilized this strange, consistent poking. I guess she will go to her grave with a formidable wooden spoon in her hand. While in her coffin, I might put some Ajax cleanser under her pillow and make sure that the round diamond ring goes in the grave too.

———·———

CHILD ABUSE CONTINUES IN MANY households around the world, and our household was no exception. In truth, my family's circumstances were not unusual. It is well known that abuse exists in wealthy homes, poor homes, revered homes, private homes, or even homes housing professional athletes. Some statistics indicate that 15.5 million children within the United States live in families in which domestic violence has occurred. An organization called Child Help indicates that a report of child abuse is made every ten seconds. They concluded that, in 2014, state agencies found an estimated 702,000 victims of child maltreatment. To imagine the astonishing enormity of those figures, consider that particular number of abused children seated in ten modern football stadiums.

My siblings and I, even with the cumulative effects of child abuse, were successful in overcoming the stigma that we placed upon ourselves. Along the way, we were able to rip ourselves from our mother's cloak and her grip over us. We carved out wonderful lives, surrounded by good and decent people. We attribute 99 percent of our demeanors to our father. And we stand as a testament to him and to other victims that we too, with determination, can live gracious lives, can move forward at a productive pace, and can cross some amazing finish lines.

Printed in the United States
By Bookmasters